WILDERNESS AS SACRED SPACE

LINDA H. GRABER

University of Minnesota

Eighth in the Monograph Series

Published by
The Association of American Geographers
Washington, D.C.

The Monograph Series of the
Association of American Geographers

Acknowledgments

The Minnesota Department of Geography provides unexcelled encouragement to its graduate students, who are treated as junior colleagues and relentlessly pushed to expand their horizons. I would like to extend special thanks and personal gratitude to my adviser, Yi-Fu Tuan, who supervised the preparation of the original version of this study as my Master's thesis, and guided my development as a graduate student in every conceivable way. Philip Porter read the manuscript and offered many helpful suggestions; fellow graduate student Ken Bowring and North Central Forest Experiment Station researcher David Lime also provided valuable comments and criticisms. David Ward's careful and insightful editorial supervision transformed this study from a rough manuscript to its present state. The experience of living in Colorado from 1967–1971, hiking its mountain trails and observing its local purists in action, helped me to formulate many of the basic interests and questions which underlie this study. Most of all, I would like to thank my husband, Lee Graber, for introducing me to the Rocky Mountain West, for endlessly discussing ideas and questions which helped us learn to perceive landscape rather than scenery, and for his unflagging encouragement and confidence that this project would be completed eventually. All credit belongs to those who have guided and encouraged my efforts; errors and omissions are, of course, my own.

Thanks are extended to the following authors and publishers for permission to quote or reproduce copyrighted material: Edward Abbey for *Desert Solitaire: A Season in the Wilderness*

(Ballantine Books, Inc., 1971); David Brower and the Sierra Club for *Going Light—With Backpack or Burro* (1951); Kenneth Clark and John Murray, Ltd. for *Landscape Into Art* (1949); Mircea Eliade and Harcourt Brace Jovanovich, Inc. for *The Sacred and The Profane: The Nature of Religion* (1961); *Aperture* for "Ansel Adams: The Philosophy of Light" by Michael Gregory (Vol. 2, No. 2, pp. 49-51, 1964), "The Photographer and The American Landscape" by Minor White (Vol. 2, No. 2, pp. 52-55, 1964), and "Review of Two Books of Photos by Eliot Porter" by John Upton (Vol. 2, No. 2, pp. 82-83, 1964); John Brinckerhoff Jackson and W. W. Norton and Company, Inc. for *American Space: The Centennial Years* (1972); William Morrow and Company, Inc. for *The Best Nature Writing of Joseph Wood Krutch* (1969) by Joseph Wood Krutch; Oxford University Press for *A Sand County Almanac and Sketches Here and There* (1969) by Aldo Leopold; Peter Smith, Inc. for *Religion in Essence and Manifestation,* Vols. 1 and 2 (1967) by G. van der Leeuw; Nancy Newhall and the Sierra Club for *Ansel Adams: The Eloquent Light* (1963); Earl Pomeroy and Alfred A. Knopf, Inc. for *In Search of the Golden West* (1957); Peter J. Schmitt and Oxford University Press for *Back to Nature: The Arcadian Myth in Urban America* (1969); Paul Shepard and Alfred A. Knopf, Inc. for *Man in the Landscape* (1967); *The Birth of Landscape Painting in China,* copyright © 1962 by Michael Sullivan, reprinted by permission of the University of California Press; Yi-Fu Tuan and the Commission on College Geography of the Association of American Geographers for *Man and Nature* (1971); Robert T. Wazeka for *The Solitary Escape in Recent American Literature* (1971); Daniel B. Weber for *John Muir: The Function of Wilderness in an Industrial Society* (1964); Jim Whittaker and Recreational Equipment, Inc. for "Lake Melakwa Clean-Up Proves Successful" in *Viewpoint* (1973); *Journal of Forestry* for "Foresters' Perception of Wilderness User Attitudes and Preferences" by John Hendee and Robert W. Harris (Vol. 68, pp. 759-762, 1970); John McPhee and Farrar, Straus and Giroux, Inc. for *Encounters with the Archdruid* (1971).

Linda H. Graber

Table of Contents

List of Figures

To L. A. G.

Introduction

Geography attempts to understand man's role in changing the face of the earth. It is a truism that landscapes are created to conform at least partially with the local inhabitants' perception of their natural environment. One mode of environmental perception, the wilderness ethic, is widespread in the United States today and shapes the management of hundreds of thousands of acres of public land, the official Wilderness Areas. It is worthwhile to examine this wilderness in detail, both in its essence and in its manifestations. The wildlife biologist Raymond F. Dasmann believes that

> Here in the United States our sense of the past, our interest in nature, our desire for outdoor recreation, and our concern for outdoor scientific study areas combine with deep and sometimes irrational emotions toward wilderness that may defy logical analysis. . . .There is a need to distinguish and separate the various reasons for advocating the preservation of wild areas. Confused emotionalism can result in confused management. Such can lead to the destruction of wilderness.[1]

I do not agree that attitudes toward wilderness defy logical analysis. There is an underlying unity to the varied and apparently conflicting arguments in favor of wilderness preservation because wilderness has become a contemporary form of sacred space, valued as a symbol of geopiety and as a focus for religious feeling. We live in a secular age, so the religious essence of the wilderness ethic tends to be overshadowed by attempts to justify wilderness preservation on secular grounds, be they scientific,

---

[1] Raymond F. Dasmann, *A Different Kind of Country*. New York: The Macmillan Company, 1968, pp. 12-13.

aesthetic, nationalistic, or hygienic. Wilderness preservation is often presented as a means to some widely desired end, rather than as an end in itself. Secular arguments in favor of a religious goal tend to be somewhat misleading, for public programs such as outdoor recreation, watershed management, or wildlife habitat preservation do not necessarily require wilderness locations to be successful. Outdoor recreation can be enjoyed on a softball diamond, watershed management is compatible with well-planned roads and resorts, and wildlife habitat can be preserved for many species in farm ponds and woodlots. The intense emotion and rigid codes of conduct associated with wilderness areas suggest a motivation beyond the practical. Whether we realize it or not, an influential portion of the American public treats wilderness as sacred space.

Many causes and interest groups tend to be lumped together by the popular press as "environmentalist," including pollution abatement, conservation of natural resources, wildlife protection, population control, land use planning, "beautification," and preservation of natural areas of outstanding aesthetic or scientific interest. Wilderness preservation is only one small aspect of environmentalism, but this study will attempt to show that the ideas, imagery, and political tactics which comprise the wilderness ethic have had a major impact on the way in which we perceive environmental problems and their solutions. Perception sets the stage for action: public programs on behalf of environmentalist goals depend on the manner in which we perceive the goal itself. The wilderness ethic has had an important impact on the form and content of American environmental goals, because the wilderness ethic is the most vital and broadly accepted contemporary expression of the search for human meaning in the landscape. What are the key ideas, value judgments, images, and political implications of the wilderness ethic? How do they find expression in the personal behavior and political activities of wilderness purists? What elements in the wilderness ethic appeal most to the public at large, and how are these elements used to mobilize public opinion on behalf of wilderness preservation and its associated environmental goals? How and to what extent do religious formulations of man's place in nature influence environmental policy recommendations made by wilderness purists?

This study will attempt to answer these questions by isolating the basic ideas of the wilderness ethic and by analyzing their role in giving form and definition to human encounters with nature. Powerful images and ideas help create an emotional and intellectual orientation toward events and thereby define experiences as much as events themselves. The wilderness ethic provides an influential segment of the American public with the means to organize and solidify those aspects of experience which involve personal interaction with the physical environment. Essentially, this study attempts to describe the logical flow from perception to experience and political action, with respect to wilderness preservation and environmental protection. It is an exploratory study, necessarily incomplete and tentative in its structure and conclusions.

The tentative quality of this study is emphasized by the questions it does not attempt to answer. First, it is neither a defense nor a criticism of the wilderness ethic. Popular and academic literature is replete with argumentative essays which justify or condemn wilderness preservation and its associated environmental goals. My purpose is to classify such arguments and to search for their underlying value judgments about man-nature relations. Second, this study is not intended to provide decision-makers with a management tool. It contains no technical insights or policy recommendations but rather examines the nature of the problems which confront decision-makers. Third, it is not a historical study. It concentrates on the experience and behavior of contemporary wilderness purists, and it relies upon reviews of the work of Roderick Nash, Hans Huth, Raymond Williams and other scholars for the necessary historical foundations. Fourth, this study does not pretend to discuss the emotions or actions of the majority of outdoor sportsmen and wilderness users. It concentrates on a small but powerful minority, the community of wilderness purists, and examines the role of this group as a political elite. Finally, this study is not empirical. This exploratory effort relies on a formal, deductive structure to fence out the many fascinating side issues which threaten to invade the argument. Once a question is clearly defined, it lends itself well to empirical testing and analysis. This study is merely a preliminary attempt to define an issue by rearranging known facts in new patterns.

To use environmental perception as the starting point for

analysis is to follow the pioneering work of geographers such as Yi-Fu Tuan, Paul Shepard, and David Lowenthal. They have established that perception of nature is culturally defined, and that the symbolic value ascribed to archetypical landscapes evolves with culture. Environmental attitudes, perceptions, and values resemble other cultural foundations in the sense that they are seldom verbalized or known by those outside a culture's educated elite but nevertheless they define and organize human orientation toward environment in many subtle ways. Religious beliefs are often expressed in symbols derived from geographical realities, such as the cosmic mountain, the garden of innocence, or the City of God. The study of symbolism is well advanced in psychoanalysis, aesthetic philosophy, and history of religions and to a growing extent, the works of Carl Jung, Ernst Cassirer, Susanne K. Langer, Mircea Eliade, and Gerardus van der Leeuw are being used by geographers, anthropologists, and other social scientists for insight into human motivation and behavior. Murray Edelman in particular has done much to apply the study of symbolism to questions of political arousal and quiescence which are central to this study. Finally, it is impossible to consider the relations between American culture and landscape changes without immersing oneself in the work of John B. Jackson. Jackson has illuminated the historical and social context of the evolving relationships among American environmental ideals, landscape development, architecture, landscape architecture, and planning.

The following discussion is divided into three major sections. Chapter I, "Sacred Space and Geopiety," uses concepts derived from phenomenology of religion to consider the wilderness ethic as a belief system, and wilderness purists as a community of believers. This section attempts to define key terms, to establish the nature and characteristics of sacred space, to describe the fundamental assumptions about man-environment relations which underlie the wilderness ethic, and to sketch the social characteristics of the community of wilderness purists. Chapters II and III consider patterns of interaction between the belief and the believer; the object and subject in reciprocal relation. "Inward Action" considers the process by which individual experience is generalized to a group mode of perception by means of the development and dissemination of wilderness imagery. Verbal and visual images lend "significant form" to individual feelings, and help define the wilderness experience as an event central to one's inner life. "Outward Action" discusses the political implications of inward action. Individual behavior in wilderness and group political action on behalf of preservationist goals are shown to be dependent on wilderness imagery for conceptual definition and for public visibility. Chapter IV presents a summary and conclusions, in the form of six themes which characterize the wilderness preservation movement as a belief system and as a political program.

I

Sacred Space and Geopiety

I n order to grasp fully the idea of sacred space, it is essential to separate religious experience from the activities of religious institutions. The former is a sudden illumination of individual consciousness, believed by mystics to be caused by personal contact with sacred power; the latter perform social functions, such as contributing to the maintenance of group identity, authority, organization, and social control. Followers of an established religion may gain spiritual insight from participation in rites, belief in a theological system, or adherence to a moral code, but such participation is quite different from pure religious experience. Religious experience does not have "content;" it is not "about anything" but itself, at least to a mind in a state of transcendence. To understand how religious experience and religious institutions differ, we must examine how the human personality reacts to contact with sacred power and how sacred power reveals itself in the human context.

THE IDEA OF SACRED SPACE

The Sacred

Imagine walking through the tunnels of a uranium mine. The air you breathe and the rock beneath your feet are saturated with low-intensity radiation. It will not harm you in small doses, and without a Geiger counter you cannot prove that it exists at all. Yet your protective clothing and the film chip on your lapel demonstrate a belief in the power of uranium ore, a power simultaneously sought and feared.

Like radioactivity, sacred power is morally neutral, burning those who approach too closely. It is ultimate being and reality, unendingly enduring and effective.[1] Sacred power is different from holiness, which is usually taken to mean "absolute goodness." The foundation of religion is not ethical—that comes later—it is a sense of overwhelming Power beyond the self.[2] When a person makes contact with sacred power, we say that he has experienced the "numinous."

This term was first proposed by Rudolph Otto in *The Idea of the Holy,* his classic work on the phenomenology of religion. According to Otto, the numinous affects human consciousness in two ways: the sense of "creature-feeling" and the awareness of *mysterium tremendum.* "Creature-feeling" implies that in the presence of sacred power, one feels like a created thing made of clay: fragile, transient, and almost formless in comparison with absolute might. *Mysterium tremendum* is a composite of many varieties of the feeling of mystery. *Tremendum* has three elements. "Awefulness" is the fear of God, a wonderful shudder of apprehension. *Majestas* is overpoweringness and regal authority. Urgency is the third element in *tremendum,* because the numinous is full of energy and dynamism. *Mysterium* is composed of two elements: the Wholly Other and fascination. The concept of the Wholly Other may be one of Otto's most enduring contributions to the vocabulary of religious psychology. Sacred power is completely different from our ordinary profane experience, separate and alien beyond human knowing. Therefore, the second element of *mysterium* is fascination. The Wholly Other attracts and repels simultaneously, but whatever the mood, a mind in the grips of numinous experience desires to keep contact as long as possible.[3]

Contact with sacred power is a self-transcending experience which carries the mind to the edge of its limited plane of understanding. Nevertheless, religious experience takes place in the context of the specific, objective world around us.[4] Religious

---

[1] Mircea Eliade, *The Sacred and the Profane: The Nature of Religion.* New York: Harper Torchbooks, 1961, pp. 12-13.
[2] Rudolph Otto, *The Idea of the Holy: An Inquiry Into the Idea of the Divine and Its Relation to the Rational.* London: Oxford University Press, 1925, pp. 6-7.
[3] *Ibid.,* pp. 8-41.
[4] G. van der Leeuw, *Religion in Essence and Manifestation.* Gloucester, Mass.: Peter

experience occurs within the mind, yet the outer world gives the experience its form and its vocabulary of feeling. Feeling is not possible without speech and gesture, thought is not present without form and action, and even mysticism requires words.[5] Sacred power is apprehensible by the human mind through the medium of concrete objects, events, persons, and places.

Hierophany: Manifestations of the Sacred

Mircea Eliade introduced the term "hierophany," meaning "something sacred shows itself to us." Hierophanies occur when something of a Wholly Other order shows itself in objects that are an integral part of our natural profane world. The primitive's sacred stones and trees are not venerated for themselves, they are worshiped as hierophanies.[6] "By manifesting the sacred any object becomes *something else,* yet it continues to remain *itself,* for it continues to participate in its surrounding cosmic milieu."[7] Any object can become a hierophany through the power of religious experience.

To the religious mind, all nature is capable of revealing itself as cosmic sacredness. Nature itself is not worshiped, but the Power that reveals itself in nature. Worldwide, mountains have been regarded as seats of Power, Wholly Other from the garden on the plains. Huge trees have been regarded as evidence of the unity of the cosmos, with roots in the underworld, the trunk on earth, and branches in the heavens.[8] Nature is never merely "natural." It is a divine creation filled with religious value: the different modalities of the sacred are manifest in the structure of the world.[9]

Nature as a manifestation of the sacred has been well described by John Ruskin in an account of his own numinous experience.

> . . .although there was no definite religious sentiment mingled with it, there was a continual perception of Sanctity in the whole of nature, from the slightest thing to the vastest; an instinctive awe, mingled with delight; an indefinable thrill, such as we sometimes imagine to indicate the presence of a disembodied spirit. I could only feel this

Smith, 1967, p. 462.
[5] *Ibid.,* p. 459.
[6] Eliade, *Sacred and Profane,* p. 11.
[7] *Ibid.,* p. 12.
[8] van der Leeuw, *Religion in Essence,* pp. 23-58.
[9] Eliade, *Sacred and Profane,* p. 116.

perfectly when I was alone, and then it would often make me shiver from head to foot with the joy and fear of it. When often being some time away from the hills I first got to the shore of a mountain river. . . or when I first saw the swell of distant land against the sunset, or the first low broken wall covered with mountain moss. I cannot in the least describe this feeling. . .the joy of nature seemed to me to come from a sort of heart-hunger, satisfied with the presence of a Great and Holy Spirit. . . .These feelings remained in their full intensity til I was eighteen or twenty, and then, as the reflective and practical power increased and the "cares of the world" gained on me, faded gradually away, in the manner described by Wordsworth in his "Intimations of Immortality."[10]

Sacred Space

Space is not a homogeneous mass, nor a sum of innumerable parts. Localities are like instants in time: specific, independent, unique. Space becomes place when man selects a "position" from the vast extent of the world, occupies it, and "takes a stand." In this way man recognizes the power of a locality and treats it as he perceives it, to be avoided or cherished, strengthened or enfeebled.[11] Some parts of space are wholly different from others. Sacred space is exceptionally strong and impressive, making profane space seem formless in comparison. When the sacred reveals itself in space, man gains a fixed point of orientation in the chaotic relativity of the profane world. Sacred space is the site of power, and makes itself known by the effects of power repeating themselves there, or by the effects of power being repeated in ritual by man. Man clings with obstinate tenacity to sacred sites once they are revealed, as may be seen in the frequent location of Christian churches on the sites of pagan shrines.[12]

Almost all levels of culture have separate, dedicated, fenced, hallowed spaces. Sacred space fascinates and attracts, but fear of sacred power adds an element of absolute unapproachability. Ritual attempts to resolve this conflict by setting rules on whom may approach, when, how, and so on.[13] Sacred space must be approached with respectful caution not only because of its

[10] John Ruskin, in van der Leeuw, *Religion in Essence,* p. 393.
[11] Eliade, *Sacred and Profane,* pp. 20-22.
[12] van der Leeuw, *Religion in Essence,* p. 393.
[13] Erich Isaac, "God's Acre," in *The Subversive Science: Essays Toward an Ecology of Man,* Paul Shepard and Daniel McKinley (eds.). Boston: Houghton Mifflin Company, 1969, p. 151.

awesome mood, but also because it is the site of a "break in plane." It is a free-fire zone for Heaven, a place for ontological passage from one mode of being to another. To enter sacred space is to request religious experience.[14]

Geopiety

Geopiety is a subset of sacred space: the Church of the Nativity in Bethlehem is sacred space, but it does not exemplify geopiety for it does not direct worship toward the earth itself. Geopiety is an aspect of religious feeling with connotations of reverence, propitiation, affection, and compassion.[15] This constellation of emotions is pantheist in effect, with the same worshipful attitude being directed toward earth as toward sacred power. Earth is seen as one vast hierophany, but since a planet is too much for our weak imaginations, sites are selected for special attention (Figure 1). The Roman *genii loci* were examples of

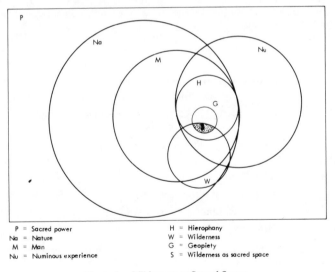

P	= Sacred power	H	= Hierophany
Na	= Nature	W	= Wilderness
M	= Man	G	= Geopiety
Nu	= Numinous experience	S	= Wilderness as sacred space

Figure 1   Wilderness as Sacred Space

[14] Eliade, *Sacred and Profane*, p. 63.
[15] Yi-Fu Tuan, "Geopiety," unpublished manuscript. Univeristy of Minnesota, Department of Geography, 1972. (Photocopied.) Edited version later published in *Geographies of the Mind: Essays in Historical Geography in Honor of John Kirtland Wright,* David Lowenthal and Martyn J. Bowden (eds.). New York: Oxford University Press, 1975, pp. 11-39.

geopiety, with human worship directed toward the spirit or character of a place. The Earth Mother goddesses of the ancient Mediterranean religions are another example.

Man and the Sacred

Ancient religious man is thought to have enjoyed a unified cosmos, where institutional religion, society, and economic life were one. Man felt that all his doings were rooted in cosmic order, giving a complete and fulfilling attitude toward life which many believe is now lost. Religious man attempts to live a sacred life in sacred space, which is the same for him as living in the center of reality.[16]

In contrast, profane life in profane space paralyzes modern man with its chaotic relativity. No true orientation is possible, the fixed point appears and disappears as convenience dictates.

> Properly speaking, there is no longer any world. There are only fragments of a shattered universe, an amorphous mass consisting of an infinite number of more or less neutral places in which man moves, governed and driven by obligations of an existence incorporated into an industrial society.[17]

Experience of a radically desacralized Nature is a new discovery of the human spirit, limited in its intense form to the scientifically educated minority. For others, nature still exhibits a charm and an appeal, which are weak sensations indeed compared to the primordial awe our ancestors experienced. In our response to the charms of nature one can find faint traces of ancient religious values. The aesthetic, recreational, and hygienic values attributed to nature are mixed with confused remnants of religious feeling.[18]

Crypto-religious behavior toward places lingers on as well. Modern man has privileged places such as his hometown or the scene of his first love.

> Even for the most frankly nonreligious man, all these places retain an exceptional, a unique quality; they are the "holy places" of his private universe, as it were in such spots that he has received the revelation of a reality other than that which he participates in through his daily life.[19]

[16] Eliade, *Sacred and Profane*, p. 28.
[17] Ibid., pp. 23-24.
[18] *Ibid.*, pp. 151-152.
[19] *Ibid.*, p. 24.

A purely rational man is an abstraction never found in real life. Much of our existence is fed by impulses that come from the zone which has been called the unconscious. Historically, religions have provided outlets for unconscious energy, channeling it into socially useful actions through moral interpretations of sacred power. When religion is weak or corrupt, irrational experience overflows its banks. Pseudo-religions and debased mythologies, such as Nazism, use inherited forms to mobilize the unconscious energy of a population to achieve dubious political goals.[20]

The Christian churches of the eighteenth and nineteenth centuries made a poor strategic decision when they set faith in the literal interpretation of the Bible against science. We live with the consequences today. In the United States today, sophisticated churches bow to science and no longer demand word-for-word belief. In the process, they have lost touch with the sense of sacred power which is the foundation of religion and have become noble ethical husks. The fundamentalist churches still cling to the authority of the Bible and are intensely aware of sacred power, but their tenets seem absurd to the educated classes. Fundamentalists seem unaware of the incompatibility between their literal and literal-minded interpretation of the Bible and the concept of sacred power as overwhelming—overflowing the constraints of words and images.

Modern men with secular educations desire and seek numinous experience in much the same manner as their ancient ancestors. The goal is the same, but the preferred path to enlightenment varies among cultures and over time. Over the past decade the United States has experienced an experimental period, as witnessed by the surge of popular interest in consciousness-expanding drugs and mutations of Eastern religions. A modern form of geopiety also seems to be a component of this religious experimentation. Contemporary geopiety puts man in touch with sacred power through the hierophany of wilderness as sacred space.

THE OBJECT OF GEOPIETY: WILDERNESS AS SACRED SPACE

From the 1880's to the present, many writers have noted the crypto-religious behavior of the conservation movement in

[20]*Ibid.,* p. 209.

general and the wilderness preservation movement in particular. Usually, writers use religion as a metaphor rather than as an explanation. As David Lowenthal puts it:

> A new religion is in the making. Worshippers of nature exhort us from the pulpits of countless conservation societies and Audubon clubs; the President's Advisory Commission on Outdoor Recreation transmutes their dogma into national policy; *Life* magazine gives the subject a four-color imprimatur. Nature is wonderful, we are told; pay homage to it in the Wilderness. . . .[21]

The title of a typical pro-preservation editorial reads, "Kick the Exploiters Out of the Wilderness Temple."[22] The former Executive Director of the Sierra Club, David Brower, is compared to Billy Graham.[23] Examples of this kind abound.

Why does enthusiasm for wilderness carry this crypto-religious tinge? Many contemporary Americans appear to treat wilderness as if it were some sort of sacred space. Why should wilderness be chosen as sacred as opposed to, say, city sites or heroes' graves? The unsatisfactory circular answer must be that wilderness is sacred space because people have taught themselves and others to perceive it that way. Religious experience is often focused on hierophany, which changes the worshiper's perception of the once ordinary object or place. Culture predisposes worshipers to pick particular types of objects as hierophanies. To explain why one object should be more likely to be called sacred than another requires immense work in cultural history. The reader is referred to the writings of Roderick Nash and Hans Huth for insight into the cultural history of attitudes toward wilderness in the United States. Our purpose is to approach the question of sacred space through the behavior of its devotees, but before examining the behavior of wilderness purists, we must first define the wilderness ethic and elucidate its axiom and corollaries.

The Wilderness Ethic

The Wilderness Act of 1964 defines wilderness as land unmodified by human action. It is a region which contains no

---

[21] David Lowenthal, "Is Wilderness 'Paradise Enow'? Images of Nature in America," *Columbia University Forum,* Vol. 7, No. 2, Spring 1964, p. 34.

[22] Editorial, "Kick the Exploiters Out of the Wilderness Temple," *American Forests,* Vol. 68, No. 10, October 1962, p. 15.

[23] John McPhee, *Encounters with the Archdruid.* New York: Farrar, Straus and Giroux, 1971, p. 83.

permanent inhabitants, no possibility for motorized travel, and is spacious enough so that a traveler crossing it by foot or horse must have the experience of sleeping out-of-doors. It is an area "...where the earth and its community of life are untrammeled by man, and man himself is a visitor who does not remain."[24]

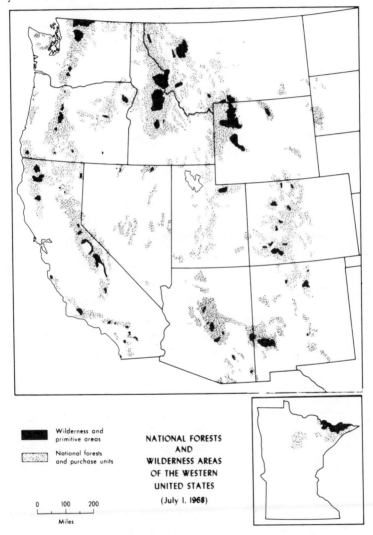

Wilderness and primitive areas

National forests and purchase units

NATIONAL FORESTS
AND
WILDERNESS AREAS
OF THE WESTERN
UNITED STATES
(July 1, 1968)

0   100   200

Miles

Figure 2   Wilderness Areas, National Forests, and Primitive Areas

[24] David Brower (ed.), *Wildlands in Our Civilization.* San Francisco: Sierra Club, 1964, p. 13.

Although wilderness inevitably conjures images of mountains, blue lakes, and conifers, it is not necessarily "scenic." Wilderness can be any type of land so long as it is unmodified, "natural," and offers opportunities for solitude[25] (Figure 2).

Absence of human beings and the consequences of their actions, then, is the definitive condition of wilderness. Sophisticated land managers feel uncomfortable about the clause "untrammeled by man." If man has been modifying the plant kingdom with fire since Paleolithic times, and if DDT is now found in the bodies of penguins in Antarctica, perhaps no place on earth can truly qualify as wilderness. In practice, however, certain human modifications are permitted in legally defined Wilderness Areas: modifications are acceptable if they are aesthetically pleasing, unnoticeable to the untrained eye, or necessary to wilderness recreation. In the National Park wildernesses, trees cannot be logged by private industry, but they can be removed to build recreational amenities such as trails. Wild animals cannot be hunted, but the equally wild fish can be taken without a fishing license. Grasses cannot be grazed by privately owned cattle or sheep, but grazing is permitted for privately owned pack stock and saddle horses.[26]

Inconsistencies of this type are not damaging, however, for the true definition of wilderness is found not in the presence or absence of physical modification, but in human needs and desires. Purists ascribe certain axiomatic qualities to wilderness. Like any axioms, the attributes of wilderness cannot be proved, but serve as the foundation of a system of thought and feeling. If one does not accept the axioms of a system, the whole structure may seem ridiculous. If one does, everything follows in an orderly and reasonable manner (Figure 3).

This system of thought and feeling may be termed the wilderness ethic. It is a permutation of modern geopiety, associated with the same urge which has made organic gardening, health foods, nudism, and "ecology" into household words. Although some criticize these popular movements as absurdly soft-headed

[25] Robert C. Lucas, "Natural Amenities, Outdoor Recreation, and Wilderness," in *Ecology, Economics, Environment,* R.W. Echan and Richard M. Weddle (eds.). Missoula, Mont.: Montana Forest and Conservation Experiment Station, School of Forestry, University of Montana, 1971, p. 145.

[26] Raymond F. Dasmann, *A Different Kind of Country.* New York: The Macmillan Company, 1968, p. 133.

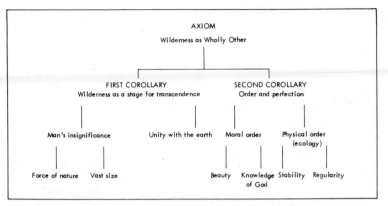

Figure 3   Axiomatic Structure of the Wilderness Ethic

or sentimental, none can deny the fervor of the adherents' beliefs, nor their sporadic success in lobbying for legislation consistent with their point of view. The wilderness ethic is the most elaborately developed version of contemporary American geopiety, with a large and well-organized group of adherents, sophisticated missionary and lobbying techniques, a major impact on the landscape, and a creative role in American culture.

The Axiom, Corollaries, and Implications of the Wilderness Ethic

The axiom of the wilderness ethic is that wilderness is a manifestation of the Wholly Other from man, and it is to be valued for that reason. This belief has major implications for its adherent's view of the proper relation of man and nature. Man is profane: the sacred power revealed in wilderness is dimmed by the presence of people and their artifacts. Unfortunately, the purist himself is human and dependent on artifacts for access to wilderness. This difficulty is overcome by rituals which set rules for proper behavior in wilderness and minimize human presence and power there.

First Corollary: Transcendence

One goes to wilderness in an attempt to transcend his ordinary world, self, and manner of perception; in other words, to have a religious experience. Man needs wilderness for its hypnotic effect (metaphorically speaking), which puts him in a receptive mood for contact with sacred power. Wilderness helps man to achieve transcendence.

The achievement of transcendence in wilderness requires two psychological breakthroughs. First, the purist must fully grasp man's insignificance in comparison to nature, which is the manifestation of sacred power. Contact with Power fills man with "creature-feeling," one of the elements in the numinous. Wilderness is void of all comforting human presence, leaving the purist exposed to nature's raw energy. The forces of nature sometimes strike with sufficient violence to reduce one to elemental physical fear. Fear is analogous to creature-feeling, and can be savored by the purist as a prerequisite for awe and wonder.[27] High country lightning storms and hailstorms, rockslides, and other exhibitions of nature's strength forcibly drive home man's nothingness, especially if one survives them long enough for contemplation! The purist cherishes his own insignificance as a condition for seeing nature as sacred power.

The vast size of wilderness also helps the purist to grasp his insignificance. The official definition of wilderness requires, in effect, that areas be large enough so that they cannot be crossed in less than a day's travel by foot or horse. The knowledge that warm and cozy civilization is far away adds to the Wholly Other atmosphere of forest, mountain, and desert. The vastness of the wilderness serves as a reminder of the vastness of the cosmos. The unexplored land beyond the crest of the next hill suggests the unknown and unknowable depths of sacred power. Vast unexplored lands are a source of fascination and attraction, but their aura of danger and otherness forces man to approach in a mood of humble caution. The purist must experience a second moment of insight if he is to achieve transcendence. Although man is insignificant in comparison to nature, he is also part of nature. The purist must reject his feelings of human superiority in favor of a pantheist-like vision of shared essence. Purists tend to believe that man's awareness of his true unity with nature is dulled by life in urban, industrial society, but a journey to wilderness helps shake off the crust of habit. It is necessary to go to wilderness for enlightenment because by definition wilderness is the best part of the earth; Wholly Other, free from man and his artifacts. "Roots in the earth" is the most frequent metaphor for this belief in pro-wilderness preservation literature. It suggests

[27] *Ibid.*, p. 144.

that man sucks up power into himself from wilderness much as plants pull nutrients in from the soil. Thoreau said it best:

> The West of which I speak is but another name for the Wild, and what I have been preparing to say is, that in Wildness is the preservation of the world. Every tree sends its fibres forth in search of the Wild. The cities import it at any price. Men plow and sail for it. From the forests and wildernesses come the tonics and barks which brace mankind.[28]

Second Corollary: Order and Perfection

The first principle of the wilderness ethic also implies that wilderness provides man with a model of perfection. Men have always identified perfection with order, and order has both moral and physical aspects. In the search for physical order, ancient man studied astronomy for insight into the cosmos. The modern purist identifies perfection with ecological order; in turn, this order is identified with the absence of man and his works. Man with his busy fingers is unquestionably the world's ecological dominant, for ". . .wherever he is found he tends to break the orderly succession of life forces and make use of the stored wealth of plants, animals, and soil for his own ends."[29] If one looks at the structure and not at the details, ecology seems to transfer some of the order of Heaven down to earth, where it is more immediate and comprehensible. Ecology is disposed to emphasize stability, another aspect of order and perfection. It ". . .recognizes change in plant and animal communities but the changes are perceived as moving toward the condition of quasi-equilibrium or climax."[30] If sacred power is manifest in a perfectly-designed earth, man-caused environmental change must necessarily remove earth from its apex of perfection to a lower state of being. Change through the natural laws of evolution and succession, on the other hand, is considered to be part of the perfect design. Thus, to enter wilderness is to leave behind the profane, changing, man-dominated world for a perfect world which is a manifestation of sacred power.

If wilderness is a model of perfection, purists feel that it implies moral order in nature as well as physical order. This view

---

[28]Henry David Thoreau, in Joseph Wood Krutch, *The Best Nature Writing of Joseph Wood Krutch.* New York: William Morrow and Company, Inc., 1969, p. 256.
[29]Yi-Fu Tuan, *Man and Nature.* Washington, D.C.: Commission on College Geography, Association of American Geographers, 1971, p. 29.
[30]*Ibid.*, pp. 28-29.

is much more specifically Christian than the primordial yearning for contact with sacred power. The vision of moral (Christian) order as manifested in the design of nature was given its first modern statement by John Ray, the seventeenth century English biologist. It was used by William Wordsworth in poetry, by the Paleyites in philosophy and theology ("no watch without a Watchmaker"), by John Ruskin in aesthetics and social criticism, and by the New England transcendentalists. Interest in natural theology is still alive in the twentieth century, although it is overshadowed by the "scientific" view, which considers the quest for "sermons in stones, books in running brooks" to be a relic of sentimental anthropomorphism.

The moral order attributed to wilderness has two implications. First, the beauty of nature is thought to suggest its moral content. This connection between the Good and the Beautiful is as old as Western thought itself. John Muir considered beauty and morality as one. He called beauty "purity" and believed that as soon as man began to tamper with nature, the quality of beauty faded and became less than perfect.[31] By definition, then, wilderness is the most beautiful—and the most moral—part of nature. Although famous in his time as a glaciologist and as a botanist, Muir believed that the scientific understanding of nature was far less important than a religious understanding,[32] and that spiritual insight was identical to the perception of beauty. Hence Muir's legacy of enthusiastic landscape description. It is the observer's ability to perceive the objective truth of sacred power manifest in nature which transforms his world of facts into a world of beauty (morality). As Thoreau said, "The perception of beauty is a moral test."[33]

The second implication is that since nature is God's handiwork, the study of its moral content provides information about God Himself. John Ruskin believed that the moral order of nature demonstrates the revealed truths of the Bible. This was a dangerous position to take at a time when science was uncovering facts incompatible with scripture. Ruskin's ideas fell from favor

---

[31] Daniel B. Weber, *John Muir: The Function of Wilderness in an Industrial Society.* Unpublished Ph.D. dissertation, University of Minnesota, 1964, pp. 109-122.

[32] Roderick Nash, *Wilderness and the American Mind.* New Haven: Yale University Press, 1967, pp. 125-129.

[33] Henry David Thoreau, in Roger B. Stein, *John Ruskin and Aesthetic Thought in America, 1840-1900.* Cambridge, Mass.: Harvard University Press, 1967, p. 91.

as belief in the literal interpretation of the Bible diminished. In contrast, Thoreau believed that God was immanent in nature, making nature a sufficient revelation in itself. The danger of transcendentalism was that by rejecting a specific creed, all the eggs of faith were held in the basket of perception. If perception failed, as it may have done for Thoreau near the end of his life, the transcendentalist visionary was reduced to a mere naturalist.[34] Wilderness purists follow Thoreau in the sense that they are intensely concerned with training themselves and others to perceive the moral order manifest in nature.

Wilderness as Eden

The wilderness ethic postulated wilderness areas as earthly versions of order and perfection, where man is best able to achieve transcendence. Wilderness represents the earth as it was in the beginning, fresh from the Creator's hands.[35] When the purist enters wilderness he comes in search of religious experience, attempting to transcend his ordinary world, self, and manner of perception. Separation from other people and exposure to the vast size and raw elements of nature help the purist to achieve transcendence by stimulating a mood of creature-feeling. The purist ascribes moral order to nature and believes that it is best revealed in the beauty of the wilderness. Nature may be overpowering, but it is not alien to human moral values.

Wilderness is the zone of perfection of the earth's surface that man can find and enter. Can we say that wilderness is a contemporary version of Eden? Eden is a garden of ease, innocence, and light work.[36] In contrast, wilderness is a place of *stürm und drang*, difficult yet ennobling. The ancient Eden represented pre-industrial man's need for a vision of ease and rustic comfort to sustain him through a life of backbreaking work. Affluent Americans have achieved physical comfort in their daily lives, so perhaps they are redefining the Edenic landscape to include challenge as well as purity. The traditional concept of Eden and the contemporary purist's concept of wilderness are identical in one important respect: the original Creation is thought to survive on a select portion of the Earth's surface.

[34] *Ibid.*, p. 92.
[35] Eliade, *Sacred and Profane*, p. 65.
[36] Tuan, *Man and Nature*, p. 25.

THE SUBJECT OF GEOPIETY: THE WILDERNESS PURIST

Wilderness is the object of contemporary American geopiety and the wilderness purist is its subject; that is, the person who postulates the attributes of wilderness, believes them, and allows them to shape his behavior. Although wilderness is an idea in the mind of the purist, the purist himself is an individual in the matrix of society. The purist's wilderness ethic is a deeply felt and rigorously developed adaptation of certain major themes in American culture, including veneration of the frontier[37] and the urge to balance the urban experience with periodic personal movements "back to nature."[38] By bringing these and other themes to a new level of intensity, purists influence the feelings and behavior of their fellow citizens and thus play a creative role in American culture. Purist values help define many of the key issues of the contemporary environmental movement, from the nature of environmental quality to the delineation of legal standards for resource development. Dynamic interaction links the wilderness ethic, the purist, and the culture in which they exist; therefore, the second step in the development of the theme of wilderness as sacred space is to examine the purist in the context of his society.

Attributes of the Purist

As a first step in identifying who is a purist and why, it is useful to begin with a bald sociological description. Wilderness purists are only one group of wilderness users, although all wilderness users hold purist attitudes to some degree. Purists differ from users in the intensity of their commitment to the wilderness ethic. The true purist is more likely to define wilderness attributes in their extreme forms than the ordinary user, and he is more willing to fight for his beliefs in the political arena. Purists are more committed to the wilderness ethic than ordinary wilderness users; in turn, users have more restrictive and specific standards for recreational quality than do outdoor recreationists who find satisfaction outside the wilderness setting.

---

[37] Roderick Nash (ed.), *The Call of the Wild: 1900-1916*. New York: George Braziller, 1970, pp. 2-3.
[38] Peter J. Schmitt, *Back to Nature: The Arcadian Myth in Urban America*. New York: Oxford University Press, 1969, pp. 3-4.

The Wilderness User

Wilderness users come from all age groups, with the 25-54 year old group in the majority and the 16-18 and 19-24 groups over-represented in comparison with the overall United States population. They are highly educated. At least 25 percent have post-graduate degrees, with sixty percent of the users coming from the top ten percent of the nation in educational achievement. Wilderness users are most likely to visit wilderness areas in small family and friendship groups, characterized by intimate relationships of spouses, children, and friends. They take about six short wilderness trips per year, spending a total of 14.5 days exclusively in wilderness. One-third grew up in rural communities, one-third in small towns, and one-third in large cities. Since World War II, however, the cityward movement has been so pronounced that the present place of user residence is predominantly urban. Seventy percent of wilderness users were exposed to the wilderness experience before the age of fifteen. Recreation patterns may be set for life in the childhood and adolescent years, when perception is most acute. Forty-four percent of wilderness users have three or more close friends who enjoy the wilderness regularly, suggesting that adult social ties reinforce behavior patterns learned in childhood. Last and very suggestive, thirty percent of wilderness users belong to at least one conservation or outdoor club. Wilderness users tend to move through a steppingstone-like political development, starting with membership in local nature appreciation groups and advancing to membership in large, national, militant conservation groups.[39] It is a common misconception to assume that wilderness users differ from other outdoor recreationists in income, expenditures, or vacation time. Although wilderness users are highly educated and hence represent the professional and managerial occupations, they are not a wealthy and leisured elite.[40]

Wilderness Purists

Purists differ from users in the degree to which they internalize wilderness attributes, as well as in their social characteristics and behavior. The purist tends to be more educated than the user, makes longer trips more frequently, and

[39] John C. Hendee, *et al., Wilderness Users in the Pacific Northwest: Their Characteristics, Values, and Management Preferences.* U.S. Forest Service, Pacific Northwest Forest and Range Experiment Station, Research Paper PNW-61, pp. 11-23.
[40] Lucas, "Natural Amenities," p. 149.

is more strongly committed to conservation organizations. Purists are more likely than users to have been brought up in urban areas and are more likely to belong to one or more organizations.[41] Perhaps because a city contains a larger pool of potential purists than a small town, they tend to find one another, organize, and reinforce each other's attitudes toward wilderness.

How do purists see themselves, and what constitutes a "wilderness experience" for them? David Brower, former Executive Director of the Sierra Club, felt that the purist is

> . . .a special sort of person, one not completely civilized, a throwback to an earlier age when man lived close to nature—his enemy if he were ignorant or slothful, his friend if he were observant, ingenious, self-reliant, and tough. Those who retain an atavistic residue like to give up the luxuries of civilization from time to time and go on a sort of spree, during which they deliberately substitute legs for wheels, muscles for motors. . .[42]

Brower's statement shows a strong respect for asceticism and for Spartan values. Immersion in an improving *milieu* is contrasted with the unmanly luxury of civilization. Those who like wilderness are special people, observant, ingenious, self-reliant, tough, and possessed of muscular legs; while those who lag behind in civilization are slothful, ignorant, and dependent on wheels and motors. There is a sense of group cohesion here, with members united in their desire to become "a special sort of person."

John Hendee identified seven characteristics which may be used to separate purists from other outdoor recreationists. Each characteristic may be described by a list of activities, likes and dislikes, and so on, which purists consider to be appropriate to the wilderness experience.

1) *Spartanism:* This is purist's most important characteristic and goal. He hopes to find in wilderness opportunity to:
   a. Improve physical health
   b. Find adventure
   c. Recapture the pioneer spirit
   d. Engage in physical exercise
   e. Acquire knowledge
   f. Learn to lead the simple life
   g. Relieve tension

[41] Hendee *et al., Wilderness Users*, pp. 22-23.
[42] David Brower (ed.), *Going Light—With Backpack or Burro*. San Francisco: Sierra Club, 1951, p. 1.

h. Attain new perspectives

i. Breathe fresh air

j. Gain emotional satisfaction

k. Get physically tired[43]

2) *Antiartifactualism:* In descending order of dislike, purists are disturbed by the presence of:

a. Campsites with plumbing

b. Equipped bathing beaches

c. Developed resort facilities

d. Gravel roads

e. Car camping

f. Automobile touring

g. Camps for organizations

h. Private cottages

i. Powerboating

j. Man-made reservoirs

k. Campsites with outhouses

l. Purchasing curios

m. Cutting Christmas trees

n. Viewing naturalist exhibits.[44]

3) *Primevalism:* Purists are delighted by:

a. Waterfalls and rapids

b. Alpine meadows

c. Timberline vegetation

d. Natural lakes

e. Virgin forest

f. Rugged topography

g. Unchanged natural coastlines

h. Native wild animals

i. Vast area and enormous vistas[45]

4) *Humility:* This might be considered to be the basic value judgment behind antiartifactualism and primevalism. In order of descending importance, purists feel that it is inappropriate to come to wilderness seeking:

a. The opportunity to boast

b. A sense of personal importance

c. The chance to stumble onto wealth

---

[43] Hendee *et al.,* *Wilderness Users,* p. 29.

[44] *Ibid.*

[45] *Ibid.,* p. 30.

    d. Wildflowers for picking

    e. Christmas trees for cutting[46]

5) *Craft aspects* of the wilderness experience are valued by purists in conjunction with Spartanism:

    a. Backpacking

    b. Hiking

    c. Mountain climbing

    d. Canoeing

    e. Sleeping outdoors[47]

6) *Aversion to social interaction:* Purists have little patience with:

    a. Hearing naturalist talks

    b. Viewing naturalist exhibits

    c. Studying pioneer history

    d. Talking with tourists[48]

7) *Escapism:* Purists have very positive attitudes toward:

    a. Remoteness from cities

    b. Absence of man-made features

    c. Solitude

    d. Vast areas and enormous vistas

    e. Tranquillity[49]

In short, purists seek a Wholly Other environment from their daily urban surroundings and oppose the penetration of reminders of the ordinary world into wilderness. The seven characteristics described above outline an extraordinarily complete set of dicta on what is proper in the wilderness setting, how one should treat wilderness, and why. Ordinarily, one would assume that the highly educated purists would enjoy absorbing information, but since the presentation of information requires naturalist lecturers and display facilities, information too must be sacrificed. The U. S. Forest Service researchers quoted earlier were disappointed by the sixth characteristic of purists and especially by a. and b. They suggested that purists object to the means of information presentation (talking, viewing, hearing) which involve dependence on an authority figure and special display facilities, but not to the end of information presentation

---

[46] *Ibid.*
[47] *Ibid.*
[48] *Ibid.*
[49] *Ibid.*

itself.[50] As the antiartifactualism section demonstrates, purists dislike aids to "roughing it smoothly" along with those who use them. Purists tailor their behavior, goals, and attitudes toward the axiom of the wilderness ethic, that wilderness is to be valued precisely because it is free from human influence.

Wilderness Purism as an Urban Phenomenon

Wilderness purists are far more likely to have been brought up in urban areas than ordinary wilderness users. The city-dwelling nature lover as a social type is almost as old as the city itself.

> We owe to the city our aesthetic appreciation of nature: directly because it is in the city that artistic sensibility is cultivated; indirectly because to be keenly aware of something we need to have its antithesis, and the city is the antithesis of nature. . . .Through the millennia of written history we repeatedly find sentiments for nature expressed in reaction to the failings of urban life.[51]

In the past, the artistic and upper class rebound from the city led not to the farmstead but beyond it to nature.[52] The upper class aesthetic view of nature condescends to the farmer and tends to take for granted the dependence of both city and country on the agricultural base. Despite traditional American regard for the small family farm, wilderness purists often bring a similar disregard to the problem of rural livelihood; for example, the contrast between characteristic urban and rural attitudes toward private property illustrates part of the difference between two environmental ideals. City dwellers are prone to regard open land as common land and tend to use it as they would a National Forest. Only land surrounding buildings is regarded as truly private. In contrast, rural landowners tend to regard property as wholly and sacredly their own, with no public rights.[53]

When urban wilderness users pressure government to reserve yet another wilderness area, rural landowners often perceive this action as an implied threat to their property rights: if potentially productive public lands may be reclassified as wilderness for the benefit of city recreationists, might not adjacent private lands be next? In addition, many rural Western landowners depend on access to public lands for livestock grazing and timber supplies.

[50] *Ibid.*
[51] Tuan, *Man and Nature*, p. 34.
[52] *Ibid.*
[53] Dasmann, *Different Kind of Country*, p. 87.

In the heat of political battle, purists may perceive local senti-ment in favor of resource development as philistine tunnel vision. This mutual antagonism adds a great deal of bitterness to political controversies over the reservation of recreational lands, as demonstrated in the Redwoods[54] and North Cascades[55] Na-tional Parks controversies. (Park supporters "won" in both cases.) Dasmann suggests that since city dwellers now have the political power to make decisions about wilderness, they should begin to bear more of the indirect costs of its maintenance. Although wilderness areas are administered by the U. S. Forest Service and hence supported by federal taxes, wilderness area reservation removes land from a rural county's tax potential. Dasmann suggests that some form of reimbursement by cities through the federal governement might be appropriate.[56]

The Community of Purists

The sacred community is a basic idea in religion. It is a brotherhood of initiates, united by shared beliefs and socially separate from the uninitiated majority. This distinction is com-mon to civilized and to primitive religions, as well as to fraternal organizations which imitate religious structure. To join the Masons, a Christian church, an ancient Roman mystery religion, or the Girl Scouts, the potential member must go through a sequence of study and activity under the guidance of an initiate. Study imbues the acolyte with the order's faith and code of behavior. When his views are uniform with his order's, he is ready for initiation.

The striking uniformity of wilderness purists' beliefs, their membership in conservation organizations, their sense of identity, and their degree of emotional commitment suggest the emergence of something like a sacred community. Sacred com-munities help their members to refine and to understand their religious experiences by sharing them with others,[57] and the comforting presence of like-minded persons helps the individual to achieve the state of mind he seeks. If the community has

[54] T.R. Vale, "Objectivity, Values, and the Redwoods," *Landscape,* Vol. 19, Winter 1970, pp. 30-33.
[55] John M. Kauffman, "A Place for a Park," *Journal of Forestry,* Vol. 66, July 1968, pp. 533-536.
[56] Dasmann, *Different Kind of Country,* p. 93.
[57] van der Leeuw, *Religion in Essence,* p. 459.

earthly goals, organization helps smooth the path to their achievement.

Sacred communities often have cultural hearths, the places in which they first appeared and which helped to shape their world view. Christianity is colored by its origins in Roman Palestine, with its administrative structure modeled after the bureaucratic hierarchy of the Roman Empire. Wilderness purists appear to have three American cultural hearths: New England, the San Francisco Bay area, and the Taos/Santa Fe region of northern New Mexico. All three regions have been long and heavily settled, but this fact does not contradict their ability to serve as foci for the development of the wilderness ethic. The regional urban centers—Boston, San Francisco, and Santa Fe—all have a distinct and often-praised sense of place which is augmented by each city's relative proximity to mountainous and lightly settled country: northern New England, the Sierra Nevadas, and the Sangre de Cristos, respectively. The cities acted as intellectual and artistic centers; the distinct city-wilderness contrast characteristic of each may have challenged local writers and artists to define the relationship of the two opposed environments. The resulting works were influential in forming the characteristic attitudes toward the region held by educated persons both locally and in other parts of the nation.

The New England transcendentalists made the definitive statement of American geopiety, but in California Nature was refined into wilderness through the influence of John Muir, who was closely identified with the transcendentalist movement. Muir's glorification of Yosemite fell on fertile soil in the San Francisco of the 1880's and 1890's. J. B. Jackson points out that in this period

> Within a hundred mile radius of San Francisco a transplanted East had evolved. . .Whatever educated circles in the East thought and did, educated circles in the Bay Region were prompt to think and do.[58]

San Francisco's ability to echo the East coast was aided by the large number of transplanted New England families, whose fathers had come to California during the Gold Rush and had stayed to prosper in commerce and industry. Some of the spirit of turn-of-the-century San Francisco is recorded in the biography

[58]John B. Jackson, *American Space: The Centennial Years, 1865-1876*. New York: W. W. Norton and Company, Inc., 1972, p. 182.

of Ansel Adams, the internationally renowned landscape photographer. Adams was born in 1904 to a prosperous upper middle class San Francisco family with roots in New England.[59] His early photographic work illustrated the *Sierra Club Bulletin,* and he served on the Club's Board of Directors since the 1930's. Several volumes of his photographs were published by the Sierra Club, including *This Is The American Earth* and his biography, *Ansel Adams: The Eloquent Light.* As a young man Adams dedicated himself to photography and music. He was friendly with the poet Robinson Jeffers and worked with him in Carmel. (Wilderness writers often quote Jeffers' lines as a summary of their views, and the Sierra Club published a folio of photographs of the Big Sur illustrating some of Jeffers' most well-known works.) By the mid-1920's Carmel had developed into a full-blown artist's colony.[60]

Jackson suggests that the California reverence for wilderness was further stimulated by the impact of large-scale corporate agriculture on the landscape of late nineteenth century California. Boom-or-bust wheat planting created a dull rural landscape and society which compared poorly to the city and wilderness environments.

> In the Central Valley of California. . .the fateful break between office and plant, white collar and blue collar, brain and hand, [was] accomplished a full century ago. Disdain for the dull workaday utilitarian countryside became characteristic of a peculiarly California environmental philosophy; a philosophy which to this day persists in seeing two, and only two, significant objects in the world: the city and the wilderness.[61]

Taos and Santa Fe may constitute a third cultural hearth for the community of wilderness purists. Taos and Santa Fe were thriving artist's colonies by 1898, attracting artists and writers from both the East and West Coasts. The painter Georgia O'Keefe arrived in 1929. D. H. Lawrence and Mary Austin, the writer and the art patroness, discovered Taos around the same time.[62] Adams arrived in Taos in the early 1930's to work with Austin on a folio of photographs and interpretation of the Taos

[59] Nancy Newhall, *Ansel Adams: The Eloquent Light.* San Francisco: Sierra Club, 1963, pp. 13-34.
[60] *Ibid.,* p. 110.
[61] Jackson, *American Space,* p. 110.
[62] Van Deren Coke, "Taos and Santa Fe," *Art in America,* May 1953, pp. 44-47.

area. Taos and Santa Fe became internationally known not for the products of native genius, but for sophisticated interpretations of local culture and landscape made by transplanted artists and writers. Much of their work was devoted to the development and celebration of the northern New Mexican sense of place, and to the extent that this sense of place depended on wilderness surroundings, artists and writers helped to develop the wilderness ethic. A spirit of place celebrated by such a talented artist as Georgia O'Keefe can become a model of excellence for other places to her admirers.

Outsiders

The community of purists stands apart from uninitiated outsiders. Discussion of who is an outsider and why helps to clarify the nature of the community of purists. Outsiders may be defined as the majority of outdoor recreationists who do not share the purist's overriding concern with wilderness. The purist is intensely aware that he holds a minority view, and his attitude toward the outsider is an unstable mixture of dislike for the outsider's "inferior" form of perception, uneasiness over his numbers and political power, and a missionary spirit which hopes to elevate the outsider to the purist's own level. As Brower said,

> There are people. . .who cannot comprehend. . .voluntary surrender of civilized comfort; people who see a mountain chiefly as an obstacle for a highway or a desert as worthless real estate; people who buy their fun instead of making it.[63]

Brower might have said that the outsider's version of fun lacks higher seriousness. Although the purist thoroughly enjoys his wilderness outings, the wilderness experience has more in common with the intelligent appreciation of an art form than it does with "whoop-it-up" fun.

In contrast, the outsider's response to the purist may take three forms: 1) ignorance of the purist's existence, 2) annoyance when purists attempt to restrict the outsider's activities, and 3) condescending tolerance, where the purist is viewed as a species of local fauna. Lucas found that powerboaters in the Boundary Waters Canoe Area of Minnesota enjoyed the sight of paddling canoeists because they complemented the scenery, but the

---

[63] Brower, *Going Light,* p. 2.

canoeists were offended by the sight of powerboaters, who destroyed the wilderness mood.[64]

Few studies exist on the question of what type of person is likely to prefer conventional outdoor recreation to purism. Although a high level of education and upper middle class status are associated with purism, not all members of this group become purists. A few small-scale studies hint at possible sociological differences. Lucas's study of littering behavior in the Boundary Waters Canoe Area of Minnesota found that males, young adults, large families, and residents of smaller communities were more likely to litter than females, older persons, small families, and city people. Residents of northeastern Minnesota were most likely to litter. Organized groups and groups led by an outfitter tended to obey antilitter regulations better than individuals or small family groups. Among types of wilderness recreationists, paddling canoeists were least likely to litter and were most offended by the sight of other people's litter. The various occupational groups were equally aware of the regulations, but obedience varied. Operatives (welders, meat cutters) and craftsmen were not particularly disturbed by the sight of litter and frequently contributed their share. Managers, professionals, and students were most likely to be offended and most likely to pack out their debris, and salesmen occupied an intermediate position.[65] Another study found that rural male residents of a recreational area preferred hunting and fishing to outdoor activities which emphasize passage (hiking, swimming, canoeing) or appreciation (nature or bird walks).[66] These findings are suggestive, but are too sketchy to categorize the outsider.

Purists and outsiders may be separated *a priori* by their attitudes toward scenery and fun. The purist has an emotionally intense, intellectually complex (and often contradictory) attitude toward wilderness. The outsider is not particularly interested in wilderness as wilderness; he seeks scenery and an outdoor playground. The outsider judges views according to an unconsciously

[64] Robert C. Lucas, "Wilderness Perception and Use: The Example of the Boundary Waters Canoe Area," *Natural Resources Journal,* Vol. 3, 1964, pp. 394-411.

[65] Stephen F. McCool and L.C. Merriam, Jr., "Factors Associated with Littering Behavior in the Boundary Waters Canoe Area, Minnesota Forestry Research Note, No. 218, 1970.

[66] S.J. Maddock *et al.,* "Rural Male Residents' Participation in Outdoor Recreation," U.S. Forest Service Research Note, SE-49, 1965.

held set of pictorial rules deriving from landscape painting. The purist is somewhat freer from the visual cliché of scenery through his intense involvement with the idea of wilderness. The outsider defines natural beauty as the closest approximation he can find of a conventional pictorial ideal. The purist defines natural beauty as freedom from human influence, and his pictorial criteria are somewhat more varied and/or austere. The contrast between outsider and purist comes into sharper focus when their ideas of fun are compared. The two groups have almost diametrically opposed views on what constitutes outdoor fun, with the outsider leaning toward a special type of social intercourse and the purist leaning toward solitary transcendent experience.

John Hendee has contributed the useful concept of the "social campground," a new phenomenon born of the self-contained camper vehicle. Traditional camping (backpacking, canoeing) is a solitary environmental encounter in the wilderness. In contrast, the developed campground is a stage for a type of social encounter. Social campers now constitute the majority of all outdoor recreationists, and thus are able to translate their ideal into recreational facilities. The developed campground may be supplied by either the public or the private sector. It consists of a landscaped parking lot with electric and sewerage hookups for camper vehicles, picnic facilities, and toilet facilities. The more desirable campgrounds include a view, a swimming pool or beach, trails, and a children's playground.

The social campground is attractive because special rules of behavior apply within its boundaries. One is expected to speak with neighbors in friendly initial encounters. A weekend wave of social campers develops rapidly into a micro-community. Social campers find the opportunity to meet new people so rewarding that contacts made in the campground are sometimes followed up in the city. The atmosphere of trust in one's homogeneous group of fellow campers lends an ease of social interaction which campers may miss at home. The generations seize on social camping as a rare opportunity to mix informally, but the expense of a camper vehicle and the ambience of the campground limit social contact with undesirables. In short, social campers are interested in one another rather than in nature, using the outdoors as a pleasant backdrop for friendly contact.

Recreation managers and campground designers tend to have an environmental orientation resembling the purist's more than the outlook of their clients, the social campers. Campground rules attempt to promote each vehicle's solitude in nature. Campsites are limited to one family, which prevents new friends from parking their vehicles in cozy proximity. Rules tend to be sacrificed to the customs of the social campground when the manager is out of sight. Water skiing in the swimming area, camping in unauthorized locations, bicycles on trails, motorscooters everywhere, unleashed dogs, and late night singing disturb the manager and please his clients. Hendee believes that the social campground should be recognized for what it is and designed to promote the enjoyment of its users. For example, campsites should encourage the formation of micro-communities and should be located near playground equipment. Since social campgrounds are almost independent of nature, Hendee suggests that they be built away from areas favored by purists. Every effort should be made to prevent conflict by segregating the two groups.

Recreation managers and purists both tend to use social camping as a synonym for low-quality recreation. In *The Wilderness User in Three Montana Areas,* Merriam describes a hierarchy of excellence in recreation, with the social camper at the bottom and the lonely mountaineer at the top.[67] In 1952 Brower believed that the Yosemite back country would remain forever inviolate, because

> The crowd diminished according to the square of the distance from the highway and according to the cube of the elevation above it.[68]

"The crowd" has a flavor of unworthiness, left behind by the purist through its inability to cope with distance and elevation. Hendee speculated wistfully on the possibility of leading social campers to a higher perception of nature.[69] The worthiness of social camping as opposed to wilderness recreation is a problem without solution because of the fundamentally different goals of the two groups. Conflict arises between social camper and purist because incompatible activities compete for the same territory.

[67] L.C. Merriam, Jr. and R.B. Ammons, *The Wilderness User in Three Montana Areas.* St. Paul: School of Forestry, University of Minnesota, 1967, pp. 38-39.
[68] Brower, *Going Light,* p. x.
[69] Hendee *et al., Wilderness Users,* p. 16.

Each group would like to enlarge its share at the expense of the other, but the supply of recreational land is finite.

Religious movements tend to have a characteristic pattern of interaction between the believer and his beliefs. Pure religious experience has no "content;" the interpretations of religious experience made after the fact, the type of follower the interpretation attracts, the manner in which followers institutionalize the interpretation in imagery, rite, theology, moral directives, and organizational goals are all culture dependent superstructures on a personal experiential base. The community of wilderness purists interprets religious experience in terms of geopiety; this orientation makes possible a wilderness ethic formally based on an axiom of belief and its corollaries. The achievement of formally stated beliefs is only part of the transition between personal religious experience and the creation of group religious institutions; the growth of the community and the achievement of its goals require powerful imagery as well as political tactics to summarize and evoke beliefs. The extraordinary success of the community of wilderness purists in generating such imagery and tactics will now be examined.

II

Object and Subject in Reciprocal Relation: Inward Action

W ilderness is the object of contemporary American geopiety and the wilderness purist is its subject. An "object" is a focus or center of attention for its "subject." As a subject perceives, considers, and acts upon his object, he experiences the object, changes it, and makes it part of his own personality. Object and subject exist in dynamic interaction; this relationship takes the forms of inward and outward action by the subject. Inward action is the interplay within the subject's mind between the object itself and the subject's perception of the object. Inward action is a process of intellectual clarification and emotional intensification, leading to the emergence of the subject as an experiential center for the subject's inner life. Outward action, in contrast, is the subject's material expression of his inward action. The act of giving concrete form to inward action changes inward action itself and prepares the subject for his next new outward action. It is a developmental, or organic process: the bud, blossom, and fruit do not resemble one another in surface appearance, but they are all expressions of one process.

The relationships among object, subject, inward action, and outward action may be imagined as a multidimensional version of the Chinese symbol for the relationship of opposites (Figure 4). The white and black zones of the *yin* and *yang* symbol are intertwined yet balanced, with the S-curve of their interface suggesting the complexity of the relationship. The white dot in the

Figure 4   The Relationship of Opposites: Yin and Yang

black zone is balanced by a black dot in the white zone, suggesting the interdependence which flows from the need to define a concept against its opposite. The same point applies to the study of object-subject interactions: one must not fall into the error of separating too completely the object and subject, nor the subject's inward and outward action. They are all expressions of one process, experience, and each depends on its opposite for definition.

Inward action makes the purist's interaction with wilderness more vivid and intense: eventually inward action may culminate in the formation of powerful verbal and visual images. Such verbal and visual images are "condensation symbols,"[1] capable of summarizing and evoking a rich array of beliefs, values, and emotions. Verbal images of wilderness are developed by nature writers within the community of purists, visual images by landscape photographers. The two sets of images are mutually supportive and consistent, to a fairly high degree, and taken together may be considered the core of a mode of perception specific to the wilderness ethic.

MODES OF PERCEPTION

Our eyes and brains are not receptors of undifferentiated stimuli: what we "see" and how we see it is shaped by our

---

[1] Murray Edelman, *The Symbolic Uses of Politics*. Urbana: University of Illinois Press, 1964, pp. 6-7.

culture and by our individual preconceptions about the nature of the world. The mind may be equipped to see with any one of an infinite number of modes of perception. A mode acts as an automatic selector of experiences significant enough to be ac- knowledged by the conscious mind. For example, the purist paddling canoeist in the Boundary Waters Canoe Area appears to have a different mode of perception from his fellow outdoor recreationist, the power boater. Every rusty can seems to leap out at the canoeist to make a disagreeable impression on his eye and brain; the power boater is far less disturbed.

Perception is unstable. Modes change and blend into one another as a person participates in life's experiences. Generally, changes in perception occur slowly, but on occasion perception may shift so suddenly that one is jolted into awareness of the change. Contact with the numinous, for example, is known to cause sudden perceptual shifts[2], as may a cataclysmic event in one's personal life, conversion to a political ideology, or contact with a great work of art. Great art in particular may owe part of its disturbing power to its ability to cause sudden perceptual shifts in many minds, widely scattered in time and space.

Perception may be changed deliberately through education or propaganda. An academic discipline is a coherent way of seeing the world acquired through training. Initiation into a community of any sort, religious, fraternal, or scientific, depends on the acolyte's success in absorbing his order's perceptual mode. A large part of education consists of the achievement of voluntary perceptual shifts which require reasoning and the conscious imitation of a model of thought. In contrast, propaganda relies on forced shifts in perception triggered by overwhelming pressure on the victim's subconscious mind by means of manipulating the symbols which organize his values and emotions.[3] Only a narrow line separates education and propaganda, one which is often crossed both deliberately and inadvertently.

Every mode of perception requires intellectual content, emo- tional content, powerful images to summarize and evoke the two, and a set of outward actions appropriate to the perceived phenomena. Such complexly intertwined elements within a mode

[2] William James, *The Varieties of Religious Experience*. London: Longmans, Green and Company, 1929, *passim*.
[3] Jacques Ellul, *Propaganda: The Formation of Men's Attitudes*. New York: Alfred A. Knopf, 1965.

of perception may not be as consistent or mutually supportive as one might wish, at least in the early stages. Actively evolving modes of perception may be permeated with difficulties, contradictions, and paradoxes arising from poor agreement among their intellectual, emotional, symbolic, and active elements.[4] Acceptance of any new mode of perception requires stressful changes in one's personal behavior and sense of identity; acceptance of a rapidly evolving, internally inconsistent mode may be especially difficult for a new convert. Schools of art and literature and their circles of admirers often suffer from growing pains of this sort, which are treated with the ointment of manifestos, discussion groups, exhibits, etc. Something similar appears to be occurring within the community of purists.

The Wilderness Ethic as a Mode of Perception

The wilderness ethic is evolving rapidly in the contemporary United States, exhibiting all the difficulties, contradictions, and paradoxes associated with a changing mode of perception. The full vision of wilderness is achieved only with difficulty, requiring the purist to sacrifice his earlier viewpoints and old patterns of emotional response to nature. Edward Abbey, the nature writer, warns how difficult it is to "see" the desert wilderness without total personal commitment to the wilderness ethic.

> In the first place, you can't see anything from a car: you've got to get out of the goddamned contraption and walk, better yet crawl, on hands and knees, over sandstone and through the thornbush and cactus. When traces of blood begin to mark your trail, you'll see something, maybe. Probably not.[5]

(A similar statement might be made about the difficulty of participating fully in any intense mode of perception, such as a theological or ideological structure.)

Many varieties of response to man and nature still exist within the wilderness ethic. Sentimentality and romance, mysticism and the scientific perspective, athleticism and religious contemplation, and a host of other inconsistent responses jostle each other for supremacy within the purist's overall perception of wilderness

---

[4] Susanne K. Langer, *Feeling and Form: A Theory of Art.* New York: Charles Scribner's Sons, 1953, pp. 15-16.
[5] Edward Abbey, *Desert Solitaire: A Season in the Wilderness.* New York: Ballantine Books, Inc., 1971, p. xii.

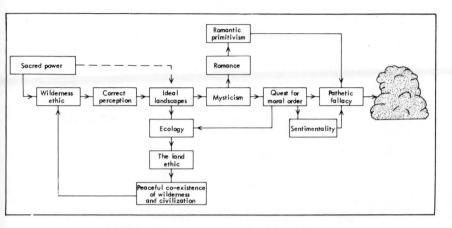

Figure 5   Varieties of Intellectual Response to Wilderness

(Figure 5). Political leaders and sensitive observers within the community of purists find it necessary to resolve these difficulties in order to arrive at a coherent group perception.

"Correct" Perception Consistent With the Wilderness Ethic

The Sierra Club's Biennial Wilderness Conferences attempt to fill the need for unity of group perception and purpose with an ongoing attempt to establish a "correct" version of the wilderness ethic. When group leaders deliberately organize conferences to develop, adopt officially, and disseminate guidelines for group perception, the perceptual mode may be said to be functioning as an ideology. Such ideology-building is extremely important, because the community of purists has political goals: purists attempt to influence government public land policy in favor of wilderness preservation and to force application of certain wilderness values to settled landscapes. Political action on behalf of the wilderness ethic is organized around verbal and visual images, which summarize and evoke the beliefs, values, and emotions which define a purist. Therefore, all attempts by the community of purists to capture the wilderness ethic in literature or art are essentially normative in character. The goal is to establish a "correct" perception, both to unify the community of purists as a political force and to unify the intellectual, emotional, and active elements of the wilderness ethic as a mode of perception. Powerful individual statements of the wilderness ethic range from expository essays on the "meaning and significance" of biological and earth sciences, to sensitive personal essays on the spiritual and aesthetic content of landscapes, to evocative landscape photography. Analysis of these verbal and visual images aids understanding of the purist's inward action, reveals certain intellectual difficulties within the wilderness ethic, and prepares the groundwork for inquiry into the political activities of the community of purists. The process of verbal image-building and its implications will be considered first.

VERBAL IMAGES: NATURE WRITING

The Role of Nature Writers in Defining the Wilderness Ethic

Nature writers struggle at the frontier of the effort to tidy up the wilderness ethic into a "correct" mode of perception. Nature writing holds an unusual place in American letters. Somewhere between science and literature, it is often regarded as ". . .no more than the eccentric outpourings of harmless hobbyists."[6] This viewpoint springs from a basic misconception of the purpose of nature writing. Its purpose is not primarily to popularize natural science by translating scientific findings into layman's language, nor even to cultivate a pure literary form. Natural science concentrates on the objective description, measurement, and prediction of various aspects of reality, with man's attitudes toward nature excluded from concern. Most literature concentrates on man's relations with his fellows, using description of landscapes and natural processes to highlight human emotions and personalities. Nature writing, in contrast, explores man's experience with nature. "Knowledge about" concerns the nature writer only insofar as it helps him to define, justify, or enrich his environmental encounters.[7]

Joseph Wood Krutch, Edward Abbey, and Aldo Leopold will be used as representative American nature writers whose stature was great enough to influence the development of the wilderness ethic. All three wrote first-person, non-fiction prose. Abbey and Krutch did their major work on the deserts of the Southwest; Leopold emphasized the Upper Midwest. Abbey was interested

---

[6] Joseph Wood Krutch, *The Best Nature Writing of Joseph Wood Krutch.* New York: William Morrow and Company, Inc. 1969, p. 265.
[7] *Ibid.,* p. 13.

primarily in wilderness, whereas Krutch and Leopold examined man's relationship with nature as a whole, with special attention to wilderness. Comparable subject matter masks a welter of personality differences, ideas, and values, which illustrates the concept of growing pains within the wilderness ethic.

Each author's tone and point of view is thoroughly compatible with his biography. Krutch was a humanist interested in the integration of man and nature. He was an elegant stylist, sprinkling his work with allusions to philosophy and literature. For many years Krutch served as a professor of English at Columbia University, as a leading New York drama critic, and as a columnist for the *Nation*. Throughout his life Krutch felt a sense of dissatisfaction with modern industrial society, fearing the results of the erosion of civilized values he believed to be occurring throughout the developed world. These misgivings were summarized in 1929 in *The Modern Temper*. In the late 1940's Krutch became interested in amateur natural science and moved from New York to the Connecticut countryside to pursue his hobby. Gradually, his interests developed beyond the hobby level. In 1952, Krutch moved to Tucson, Arizona for his health and devoted his efforts entirely to nature writing.

As might be expected, Krutch brought a humanistic, philosophical approach to nature writing which attempted to combine a light tone ("the generally now despised familiar essay")[8] with scientific accuracy. Sensation played a secondary role in Krutch's work: his theme was more likely to be an elegant description of the habits of the kangaroo rat, with a philosophical defense of wilderness woven into the narrative. Krutch's style had a slightly old-fashioned quality which pleases as much as it surprises. Because Krutch wrote in the first person, he was a character in his narrative. His *persona* was that of a cultivated older man with faith in the power of reason and in an ordered moral universe. This *persona* was maintained even when he took the most extreme positions in the justification of the wilderness ethic.

In contrast, Edward Abbey's work is extreme in tone as well as in content. He writes in a mood of bitterness and anger, forcefully presenting one point of view.[9] The anger is tempered with

---

[8] *Ibid.,* p. 25.
[9] Edwin Way Teale, "Making the Wild Scene," *The New York Times Book Review,* January 28, 1968, p. 7.

wit, self-mockery, and black humor. His style is well within the "tough" Hemingway school, occasionally achieving an excitement rare in Krutch's work. Abbey started life as a poor Pennsylvania farm boy, served in the armed forces in World War II, taught philosophy at the University of New Mexico, and later became writer-in-residence at the University of Utah. Abbey's *persona* displays contradictions which add vitality to his work. Although Abbey rejects scholarly life in favor of the "rugged" life of the seasonal park ranger, his narrative contains an attempt to build an entire philosophical system placing man in the context of the natural world. In addition, Abbey seems to have structured his *persona* to resemble Thoreau's in *Walden*.

> The trailer Abbey lives in alone at Arches [National Monument] is isolated like Thoreau's cabin at Walden Pond....Both Abbey and Thoreau cherish solitude. Both are anarchists and pacifists, although Abbey has a considerably more volatile disposition. Both rail against the ill effects of technology and overcrowding; both stress simplicity.[10]

Abbey's anger and radicalism appear to be a literary expression of the new mood in the American wilderness preservation movement. The beliefs and emotions underlying David Brower's controversial policies as Executive Director of the Sierra Club, the increased reliance on propaganda, hard-hitting political tactics, and lawsuits among purist political organizations, the emergence of clearly defined political adversaries in environmental issues, and the highly politicized and polarized atmosphere of the late 1960's all find expression in Abbey's anger, conviction, and black humor.

Aldo Leopold was born in Iowa in 1887, and began his professional career in 1909 with the U. S. Forest Service. In 1924 he became Associate Director of the Forest Products Laboratory at the University of Wisconsin. At the time of his death in 1948, Leopold was serving as an adviser on conservation to the United Nations.[11] His career coincided with the rise of scientific forestry, ecology, and wildlife management. Through his field work, research, and deeply-felt personal observations, Leopold became dissatisfied with the production-for-its-own sake attitude prevailing within his profession. Leopold was the first to suggest

[10] Robert T. Wazeka, *The Solitary Escape in Recent American Literature*. Unpublished Ph.D. dissertation, University of Colorado, 1971, p.6.
[11] Aldo Leopold, *A Sand County Almanac and Sketches Here and There*. New York: Oxford University Press, 1969, p. 1.

an ethical or religious aspect to the conservation movement, and by extension to wilderness preservation.[12] Leopold believed that economic activity would be more satisfying and stable in the long run if it were unified with the "land ethic." This unified approach was very different from the usual view which allowed economic activity to dominate most land use decisions, and ethical considerations to be served by an occasional reservation of "non-economic" lands in National Parks or Wilderness Areas.

Leopold's style combined the elegance of Krutch with the power of Abbey. His tone of practicality, experience, and competence seems to erase the usual dividing line between the "spiritual" and the "practical." Leopold saw no need to move to a higher plane when making his points: philosophy is discussed in the same tone and context as the habits of field mice. This unity of realism and philosophy gives his work an unusually solid quality. Although Krutch and Abbey are well respected by the community of purists, only Leopold has achieved the status of a latter-day Thoreau or Muir.

Each writer is closely connected with the Sierra Club, one of the most prominent purist's wilderness preservation groups. Krutch wrote a book for the Sierra Club's Exhibit Format Series entitled *Baja California and the Geography of Hope* and contributed to the 1961 Biennial Wilderness Conference. Abbey has written two books for the Sierra Club, one on Appalachia and the other on the Four Corners area of the Southwest. Leopold died before the Sierra Club began publishing the Exhibit Format Series, but he is quoted constantly in purist publications as an authority almost as important as Muir or Thoreau.

Nature writers help to define the wilderness ethic by creating verbal images which summarize its intellectual, emotional, and active components. Such verbal images are rarely limited to pure landscape description, but combine exciting narrative, field biology and earth science, argument for the value of wilderness, description of personalities, criticism of enemies and praise of friends, etc. Each author creates a somewhat different verbal image of wilderness, according to his beliefs, emotions, and personality. Nevertheless, Krutch, Abbey, and Leopold resemble one another in their preoccupation with four themes in the human response to landscape: ideal landscapes, the mystical *versus* the

[12] Roderick Nash (ed.), *The Call of the Wild: 1900-1916.* New York: George Braziller, 1970, pp. 182-199.

scientific response, the difference between sentimental and romantic responses, and the value of romantic primitivism as opposed to the possibility of peaceful coexistence between wilderness and civilization.

Varieties of Response to Wilderness

Ideal Landscapes

Many purists seem to experience a moment of transcendence when they first encounter their personal ideal landscape. This encounter thrills and shocks the purist so deeply that his perception of the landscape is changed forever: for him, it becomes sacred space. A purist's ideal landscape fascinates and attracts him to such a high degree that he may uproot his family and move to his personal sacred space. If this is impossible, he will at least visit it at every opportunity. The purist may invest a great deal of effort in defending his ideal landscape from harm, studying it for deeper appreciation, attempting to capture its mystery in art, or simply trying to communicate his delight to family and friends. Nature writers attempt to capture this moment of transcendence in their verbal images and to understand its power to transform perception.

Ideal wilderness landscapes are only one color in the rainbow of personally significant landscapes. As Abbey says,

> Every man, every woman carries in heart and mind the image of the ideal place, the right place, the one true home, known or unknown, actual or visionary. A houseboat in Kashmir, a view down Atlantic Avenue in Brooklyn, a gray gothic farmhouse two stories high at the end of a red dog road in the Allegheny Mountains, a cabin on the shore of a blue lake in spruce and fir country, a greasy alley near the Hoboken waterfront, or even, for those of less demanding sensibility, the world to be seen from a comfortable apartment high in the tender velvety smog of Manhattan, Chicago, Paris, Rio, or Rome--there's no limit to the human capacity for the homing sentiment.
> For myself I'll take. . .the canyonland, the slickrock desert, the red dust and the burnt cliffs and the lonely sky—all that which lies beyond the end of the roads.[13]

The "sand counties" and the Flambeau River of Wisconsin delighted Aldo Leopold with their diversity of plant and animal life. The small family farm coexisting peacefully with wild nature gave him intense satisfaction and formed the model for his con-

---

[13] Abbey, *Desert Solitaire*, p. 1.

cept of the land ethic. Leopold's ideal was a half-humanized landscape similar to Thoreau's Concord, where the little farms were given definition and meaning by the wilderness beyond the clearings.[14]

Ansel Adams finds his ideal landscape in the Yosemite wilderness. His first transcendental experience occurred in 1916, when he was fourteen years old.

> The first impression of the Valley—white water, azaleas, cool fir caverns, tall pines and solid oaks, cliffs rising to undreamed-of heights, the poignant sounds and smells of the Sierra. . .was a culmination of experience so intense as to be almost painful. From that day in 1916 my life has been colored and modulated by the great earth-gesture of the Sierra.[15]

Ideal landscapes often retain their power over a purist throughout his lifetime, as Adams' lifework demonstrates. Contact with the numinous may come at any time when the purist is immersed in sacred space. Adams experienced sacred power in Yosemite again at the age of 20, in 1922.

> The wordless meaning trembled on the mind's edge and passed on, while with almost hypnotic persistence, I watched the stars slowly stream over the earth. . . .There was no sentimental precedent, there was no imaginative experience with which to compare this magic actuality. My reactions spared neither my emotions nor my body; I dreamed that for a moment time stood quietly, and the vision of this actuality became but the shadow of an infinitely greater world; that I had within the grasp of consciousness a transcendental experience.[16]

Transcendental encounters with an ideal landscape may be more frequent in adolescence, when perception is most acute, than they are in later life; but are by no means limited to youth. Krutch was deeply moved by his first encounter with the Sonoran Desert of Arizona, which occurred when he was a grandfather.

> It seemed almost as though I had lived there in some happier previous existence and was coming back home. . . .The strangeness made an immediate appeal both aesthetically and spiritually.[17]

[14] Leopold, *Sand County Sketches, passim.*
[15] Ansel Adams, "Introduction" to *Yosemite and the Sierra Nevadas,* selections from the works of John Muir, Charlotte E. Mauk (ed.). Boston: Houghton Mifflin Company, 1948. Cited by Nancy Newhall, *Ansel Adams: The Eloquent Light,* San Francisco: Sierra Club, 1963, p. 29.
[16] Letter from Ansel Adams to Virginia Bush, c. 1922. Cited by Newhall, *Ibid.,* pp. 36-37.
[17] Joseph Wood Krutch, *More Lives Than One.* New York: William Sloane Associates, 1962, p. 309.

The Mystical Response

Once the purist has experienced the numinous in his ideal landscape, he begins to struggle to clarify the spiritual message he has received. Awakened awareness of wilderness as a hierophany is a message in itself, but purists frequently attempt to read a moral message in their experiences as well. The beauty of the wilderness is thought to suggest the moral order of the universe, which in turn is determined by sacred power.

The desert seems to be one of the most suggestive ideal landscapes. Its bareness appeals strongly to the ascetic temperament.[18] To Krutch, the appeal of the desert

> . . .is not the appeal of things universally attractive, like smiling fields, bubbling springs, and murmuring brooks. To some it seems merely stricken, and even those who love it recognize that its beauty is no easy one. It suggests patience and struggle and endurance. It is courageous and happy, not easy and luxurious. In the brightest colors of its sandstone canyons, even in the brightest colors of its brief spring flowers, there is something austere.[19]

It seems to Abbey that

> . . .the strangeness and wonder of existence are emphasized here, in the desert, by the comparative sparsity of the flora and fauna: life is not crowded upon life as in other places but scattered abroad in sparseness and simplicity. . .so that the living organism stands out bold and brave and vivid against lifeless sand and barren rock. The extreme clarity of desert light is equalled by the extreme individuation of desert life-forms. Love flowers best in openness and freedom.[20]

The austere beauty of the desert suggests an austere set of virtues: courage, struggle, endurance, and freedom. These human values seem to be intrinsic to the desert landscape, which is thereby elevated to sacred space. Therefore, the purist is reassured that he believes in sacred values.

Abbey and Krutch also receive a message on the unity of man and nature from their contemplation of the desert. The sense of oneness with a greater whole is a frequent occurrence in mysticism, called "the oceanic feeling" by William James. Krutch takes a keen delight in his kinship with other, non-human lives sharing the world with him.

---

[18] Yi-Fu Tuan, *Topophilia: A Study in Environmental Perception, Attitudes, and Values.* Englewood Cliffs, N.J.: Prentice-Hall, Inc., 1974, pp. 51-52.
[19] Krutch, *Best Nature Writing*, p. 75.
[20] Abbey, *Desert Solitaire*, p. 29.

. . .the acute awareness of a natural phenomenon. . .is the thing most likely to open the door to that joy we cannot analyze. I have experienced it sometimes when a rabbit appeared suddenly from a bush. . . or when, at night, a sudden rustle in the leaves reminds me of how many lives surround my own.[21]

Abbey's desire for union with the whole is proclaimed in a grotesque metaphor. Should one die of thirst in the desert,

. . .if all goes as planned, your human flesh will be working its way through the gizzard of a buzzard, your essence transfigured into the fierce greedy eyes and unimaginable consciousness of a turkey vulture. Whereupon, you, too, will soar on motionless wings high over the ruck and rack of human suffering; for the most of us a promotion in grade, for some the realization of an ideal.[22]

Although Abbey and Krutch agree on the desert as an ideal landscape, on the appeal of its austerity, and on their desire for the oceanic feeling, the above quotations reveal a certain difference in temperament. In their analysis of the desert's mystic message, the two authors differ decisively. For Krutch, the message of the desert is that nature and the human mind share one another's intentions, because both were created by God's love. In the desert, Krutch believed that nature's processes and moods corresponded to some mood he found within himself. Contemplation of the desert freed his imagination from the false man/nature dichotomy, permitting a simultaneous exploration of the self and of nature.

Perhaps the mind is not merely a blank slate upon which anything may be written. Perhaps it reaches out spontaneously toward what can nourish either intelligence of imagination. Perhaps it is part of nature and, without being taught, shares nature's intentions.[23]

Krutch's vision of the underlying unity of nature and the human mind helped him to regain his faith in humanism. Until his discovery of the spiritual renewal possible through contemplation of nature, Krutch had been trapped in his own pessimism. He believed that Marxism, Freudianism, and the shallowness of life in industrial society made individuals mere products of social forces. Since such individuals could not be held responsible for their actions, humanist values were lost. If, on the other hand, the mind reaches spontaneously toward the sacred, regardless of

[21] Joseph Wood Krutch, *The Voice of the Desert: A Naturalist's Interpretation.* New York: William Sloane Associates, 1954, p. 24.

[22] Abbey, *Desert Solitaire,* p. 274.

[23] Krutch, *Voice of the Desert,* p. 218.

social forces, individuals might achieve at least partial freedom from these forces. Because Krutch believed that the acute awareness of nature directs the mind toward sacred power, nature played a crucial role in his vision of humanism. At the same time, for Krutch nature was more than an object of contemplation; the mind and nature shared the same underlying reality. Clearly, Krutch stands within the tradition of Christian transcendentalism, where geopiety leads man toward God's love.

In contrast, Abbey's mysticism seems more akin to Taoism or Zen than to Christianity. He agrees with Krutch that the strangeness of the desert seems to promise some answer, or "great, unimaginable treasure."[24] What is this answer?

> . . .I consider the tree, the lonely cloud, the sandstone bedrock on this part of the world and pray—in my fashion—for a vision of truth. I listen for signals from the sun, but that distant music is too high and pure for the human ear.[25]

Abbey desires a vision of truth intensely, but simultaneously doubts the validity of what he will see.

> Each time I look up one of the secretive little side canyons I half expect to see not only the cottonwood tree rising from its tiny spring—the leafy god, the desert's liquid eye—but also a rainbow-colored corona of blazing light, pure spirit, pure being, pure disembodied intelligence, *about to speak my name.*
>
> If man's imagination were not so weak, so easily tired, if his capacity for wonder not so limited he would abandon forever such fantasies of the supernal. He would learn to perceive in water, leaves, and silence more than sufficient of the absolute. . .to console him for the loss of ancient dreams.[26]

The value of the desert is that its intense clarity of light and form seems to burn away the myths of theology and philosophy, leaving the landscape stripped of its overburden of human associations.

> Whirlwinds dance across the salt flats, a pillar of dust by day; the thornbush breaks into flame at night. What does it mean? It means nothing. . . .The desert lies beneath and soars beyond any possible human qualification. Therefore, sublime.[27]

Of all possible landscapes, the desert suggests the abandonment of human qualification most strongly.

[24] Abbey, *Desert Solitaire,* p. 274.
[25] *Ibid.,* p. 155.
[26] *Ibid.,* p. 200.
[27] *Ibid.,* p. 219.

> . . .The desert lies there like the bare skeleton of Being, spare, sparse,
> austere, utterly worthless, inviting not love but contemplation. In its
> simplicity and order it suggests the classical, except the desert is a
> realm beyond the human. . . .The desert waits, untouched even by the
> human mind.[28]

This rejection of human meaning resembles the Buddhist
contemplation of nothingness, in order to free the mind of all
earthly cares. This attitude implies a rejection of the value of the
human personality. The Buddhists, who reject this value, believe
that although human perception is second only to the Absolute,
it must be abandoned if union with the Absolute is to be
achieved. Although Abbey rejects the notion of human meaning
in the landscape, he stops short of the Buddhist position. Abbey
believes that the quest for human meaning in the landscape is
merely another form of human vanity, leading the observer to see
his own personality and desires rather than external reality.
Abbey's purpose in visiting the desert is to "confront the bed-
rock of existence."

> I want to be able to look at and into a juniper tree. . .and see it as it is
> in itself, devoid of all humanly ascribed qualities, anti-Kantian, even
> the categories of scientific description. To meet God or Medusa face
> to face, even if it means risking everything human in myself. I dream
> of a hard and brutal mysticism in which the naked self merges with a
> non-human world and yet somehow survives still intact, individual,
> separate. Bedrock and paradox.[29]

Abbey's paradoxical desire both to escape and to intensify his
human perception is resolved like a Zen *koan* into a new sustain-
ing ideal.

> I have seen the place called Trinity in New Mexico, where our wise
> men exploded our first atomic bomb and the heat of the blast fused
> sand into a greenish glass—already the grass has returned, and the
> cactus and the mesquite. On this bedrock of animal faith I take my
> stand, close by the old road that leads eventually out of the valley of
> Paradox.[30]

The Pathetic Fallacy and the Moral Significance of Nature

The root of the conflict between Abbey's and Krutch's styles
of contemplation is their interpretation of the "pathetic fallacy."
John Ruskin invented this term to criticize the human tendency

[28] *Ibid.*, pp. 270-272.
[29] *Ibid.*, p. 6.
[30] *Ibid.*, p. 301.

to call fields "smiling," forests "somber," or mountains "majestic." Ruskin believed that this was a false perception because man's emotional responses must be tied to the facts of nature, which are most beautiful and meaningful when seen plain.[31] Personification of nature results in a condescending sentimentality, and prevents us from learning from nature because we see only a distorted image of ourselves. At the same time, Ruskin feared the alienating dichotomy of man and nature. He believed that scientific knowledge of natural events and processes could be a source of moral sensitivity, if the facts of nature were viewed with reverence and imagination.

To what extent may moral values be drawn from landscape appreciation and natural history? Sacred power reveals itself to the purist in an overwhelming flood of new awareness: a mind in the midst of a numinous experience has no doubt of the reality of the experience. In contrast, moral interpretations of a numinous experience are made after the fact, and hence leave ample room for doubt and confusion in the purist's mind. Abbey agreed with Ruskin on the evils of personification, and valued the desert because its Wholly Other quality helped him to suppress and eliminate his tendency to personify the natural world. To Abbey, the search for moral guidance in nature is merely another form of personification: he struggled to believe that the "meaning" of the desert is that it has no moral implications. Further, the barrenness of the desert suggests the emptiness of the hope for moral guidance. This rejection of moral implications in the desert landscape bears some resemblance to the more typical purist rejection of human artifacts in wilderness. At the same time, Abbey's "animal faith" in the life force implies that he accepts at least some sort of biological relationship between himself and nature.

In contrast Krutch was not at all convinced that the pathetic fallacy was an error in perception. The ancient human tendency to personify nature through totems and fables is world-wide and by no means extinct. He believes that personification can be healthy if it is used metaphorically to underscore our unity with nature.

[31] Roger B. Stein, *John Ruskin and Aesthetic Thought in America, 1840-1900.* Cambridge, Mass.: Harvard University Press, 1967, p. 87.

[The *Reader's Digest*] has long published a continuing series of anecdotes illustrating wisdom and intelligence in animals, both wild and domestic. In this overly scientific age, many people would like to believe what primitives take for granted, that the consciousness of the beast is not essentially different from our own...this popular desire shows more generosity of spirit than the behavioral scientists who seem bent on demonstrating their own high endowments by demonstrating the absence of these endowments in all creatures except themselves.[32]

Krutch wonders whether man is in fact so separate from nature that there can be no continuity of mood.

If man comes from nature, how can the part be greater than the whole? Perhaps the joy of nature is older than the joy of man, and what is transitory here is permanent elsewhere. When the moment of happiness passes it is not that the glory has faded but that our own sight has grown dim.[33]

If nature has moral implications and if there is some sort of relationship between nature and man, it follows that man should attempt to find lessons in landscapes. Unfortunately, this attempt can easily result in a crude personification of nature, with its attendant sentimentality. Exactly what is the desert "saying?" Despite the purist's keen awareness of sacred power, he can never be sure whether he is deducing its true moral implications or merely projecting his own moral code onto his experience.

The Scientific Response

Ruskin believed that close attention to the facts of nature permits the observer to see nature's moral significance without falling into the pathetic fallacy. We usually think of mysticism as "soft" and concerned with intangibles, whereas science is "hard" and concerned with facts. The scientific and mystical responses to nature and to wilderness tend to attract different personality types with different world-views, but the two responses are not as opposed as they might seem at first glance; both search for the underlying unity of the cosmos. During the past two hundred years, the ever-increasing scope, efficiency, and precision of scientific inquiry has caught mankind's attention at the expense of "revealed" knowledge. Science seems to be abundantly justified by technology and the prosperity it brings. Given the

[32] Krutch, *Best Nature Writing*, p. 133.
[33] Krutch, *Voice of the Desert*, p. 133.

prestige of the scientific approach and outlook, many purists turn to science for the answers on the moral significance of the landscape. Since facts are objective and science is based on facts, perhaps it can supply more convincing answers than mysticism.

The search for moral guidance in nature is not the primary objective of contemporary science, although the question occurs in the work of such highly regarded scientists as Konrad Lorenz, George Wald, René Dubos, and Theodosius Dobzhansky. When science reaches its limit, the sense of awe takes hold.[34] If we use science to pry moral directives out of nature, are we using science for its highest purpose or are we falling back into an older cosmology, a relic of the heyday of the Paleyites?[35]

Aldo Leopold devoted extensive and original thought to the existence of moral directives in nature which might be uncovered through the study of biological sciences and applied to reform human social and economic institutions. According to Leopold, the science of ecology can teach man to search in animal populations for analogies to his own problems and insight on how to solve them. "The ability to perceive deeper meanings [in nature] and to appraise them critically is the woodcraft of the future."[36] The perception of "deeper meanings" in nature differs from crude personification and even from Krutch's belief in the continuation of mood from nature to man. Leopold seemed to believe in a type of physical and behavioral unity of man and nature, which is best revealed through scientific knowledge.

> It is a century now since Darwin gave us the first glimpse of the origin of species. We know now what was unknown to all the preceding caravan of generations, that men are only fellow-voyagers with other creatures in the odyssey of evolution. This new knowledge should have given us, by this time, a sense of kinship with fellow creatures, a wish to live and let live, a sense of wonder over the magnitude and duration of the biotic enterprise.[37]

Leopold's seminal contribution to the wilderness ethic was his view that scientific knowledge and mystical insight can be fused to form a "land ethic." Leopold's land ethic was simultaneously a useful mechanism which would make conservation work and a system of behavior which would bring spiritual satisfaction

---

[34] Stein, *John Ruskin,* p. 182.
[35] *Ibid.,* p. 166.
[36] Leopold, *Sand County Sketches,* pp. 194-198.
[37] *Ibid.,* p. 109.

through proper practice. One ethical system would embrace personal behavior, social relations, and all human activities that affect the earth and its community of life.

> All ethics so far evolved rest on a single premise: that the individual is a member of a community of interdependent parts. His instincts prompt him to compete for his place in that community, but his ethics prompt him also to co-operate (perhaps in order that there may be a place to compete for). The land ethic simply enlarges the boundaries of the community to include soils, waters, plants, and animals, or collectively: the land itself.[38]

The land ethic is a moral code based on geopiety. In contrast to the romantic primitivists, Leopold did not believe that wilderness and civilization were inherently incompatible. He felt that as a civilization matures, its ethical code expands and improves in a manner similar to biological evolution. The earliest ethical systems were limited in scope: the Ten Commandments, for example, regulated relations only among individuals. Eventually, in Leopold's view Western man's ethical consciousness expanded to include the individual's relations with society. Leopold believed that the third and highest level of civilization would be reached when ethical awareness expanded once again to include nature.[39] Leopold neglected to consider evidence of geopietistic codes of conduct which can be found throughout the world in all historical periods. The land ethic seemed revolutionary in the 1930's only because the prevailing land use ideology overemphasized short-run economic considerations.

Leopold's down-to-earth version of ethical theory resembles enlightened self-interest, and nothing could be farther from Abbey's mysticism. He believed that ethical growth is stimulated by new awareness of mutual dependence among members of a community. In a sense, for him human ethical systems were a more highly evolved version of the symbiotic relationships found in animal populations.[40] Thus, the land ethic was based on a moral interpretation of ecology, a science which is preeminently the study of interrelationships and mutual dependencies. Leopold believed that the study of ecology could lead to an increase in the intensity of human feeling and imagination about the natural world, the emotional basis of the land ethic.

[38] *Ibid.*, pp. 203-204.
[39] *Ibid.*
[40] Leopold, *Sand County Sketches*, pp. 194-198.

Wilderness played a special role in Leopold's land ethic. It served as a baseline to judge the relative health of domesticated lands. The undisturbed ecological balance of the wilderness could be studied for insight into the restoration of the land's health, and as a reminder and model for perfection to the professional conservationist and his citizen allies.[41]

Leopold's land ethic is immensely popular among purists because it successfully resolves four difficulties. First, the purist is encouraged to see himself as part of the advance guard for a higher level of civilization, which is a much more pleasant self-image than "nature nut." Second, Leopold's views on wilderness as a baseline fit very well with the axiom and corollaries of the wilderness ethic. Third, Leopold's fusion of the land ethic with the science of ecology lends the prestige of science to the purist's beliefs. Fourth and most important, geopietistic mystic experience gains a code of moral directives based on scientific fact, thus avoiding the pitfalls of the pathetic fallacy. Science is used to justify the purist's numinous experience and to interpret this experience as a useful, satisfying moral code.

The Sentimental *vs.* Romantic Response

The wilderness ethic is a consciously-developed style of perception resembling a "school" of art or literature. As modern literature was accompanied and partially formed by a flood of literary criticism, so the wilderness ethic is accompanied and formed by a type of perception criticism. The style and quality of wilderness perception is a source of deep concern to nature writers. One of the main themes in their work is an effort to develop standards for judgment and criticism of styles of perception.

A key problem is the separation of the sentimental from the romantic view, and the assessment of the value, if any, of romance. In general, the difference between sentimentality and romance is a question of style and scale. Sentimentality prefers the pretty, the manageable, the comfortable. Romance tends toward the sublime and challenging. The dividing line, however, is very narrow. Romantics slip into sentimentality easily, or at the other extreme into a type of aesthetic fascism, where sub-

---

[41] *Ibid.*

limity and challenge are so overdeveloped as to become brutal. In addition, romance becomes sentimental when it is a conventional, automatic response, even though it retains its interest in the large scale. As the photographer Ansel Adams said:

> Our weakness in our appreciation of nature is the emphasis placed upon scenery, which in its exploited aspect is merely a gargantuan curio. Things are appreciated for size, universality, and scarcity more than for their subtleties and emotional relationship to everyday life.[42]

Conventional romance is illustrated by the scenic lookouts constructed along roads in National Parks. Invariably the scenery is a perfect subject for a picture postcard, huge and impressive. Size and impressiveness are not liabilities; the fault lies in the implicit assumption that only size and impressiveness matter. Scenery of this type seems somehow unnatural perhaps because the lookouts were selected for their resemblance to romantic landscape art.[43]

The sentimental legacy of early twentieth century nature writing is an embarrassment to present-day wilderness purists. Because the dividing line between sentimentality and romance is so narrow, ridicule directed at sentimentality may embrace romance as well. Turn-of-the-century nature writers lacked the sophistication and scientific training of present-day writers. As a result, early writers were very fanciful in their interpretations of man's experiences with nature. They tended to write from a teleological point of view, viewing the habits of wildlife according to Victorian morality. With respect to ornithology, "good birds" had attractive plumage and songs, ate seeds or insects, built intricate nests, mated once a year, and never disturbed other nesting birds.[44] "Bad birds" were unattractive and ate carrion. The worst bird of all was the English sparrow, which fed on the undigested corn in horse manure and lived in the street, with all the implications that "the street" carried in Victorian language. With respect to mammals,

> Lobo stands for Dignity and Love-Constancy, Silverspot for Sagacity; Redruff, for Obedience; Bingo for Fidelity; Dixie and Molly Cottontail for Motherlove; Wahb the Elk for Physical Force, and the Pacing Mustang for Love of Liberty.[45]

---

[42] Ansel Adams, cited by Earl Pomeroy, *In Search of the Golden West: The Tourist in Western America.* New York: Alfred A. Knopf, 1957, p. 215.

[43] *Ibid.*, p. 155.

[44] Peter J. Schmitt, *Back to Nature: The Arcadian Myth in Urban America.* New York: Oxford University Press, 1969, *passim.*

[45] *Ibid.*, p. 47.

The impulse to see animals in human terms is as old as Aesop, and can be a delightful form of fiction. However, many early twentieth century nature writers were unconcerned about the border between fact and fiction and their readers often mistook their writings for factual natural history. In addition, this unnatural natural history tended to be "...purified of blackflies and mosquitos, frigid cold and steaming summer heat."[46] Nature was humanized and prettified until its meaning and beauty were more obvious in literature than in real life. Scientific nature writers and experienced outdoorsmen, such as Theodore Roosevelt, despised the "nature fakers" as the sentimentalists were called. Social Darwinists preferred to emphasize the brutal competition of the "struggle for existence". Nevertheless, the sentimentalist impact was great enough to leave a pink cloud over nature writing as a literary form.[47]

Popular nature writing has had a major impact on the public's developing perception of wilderness, and has influenced the views of many potential converts to the wilderness ethic. A sentimental verbal image is inconsistent with the wilderness ethic because it institutionalizes the pathetic fallacy, whereas purists perceive the sacred in wilderness because of its Wholly Other quality. Purist writers struggle to achieve an empathetic tone without falling into sentimentality. Fear of the pathetic fallacy is very marked in Abbey's work, but ironically, Abbey indulged in the grotesque pathetic fallacy to a far greater degree than Krutch or Leopold. (For example, in the remark quoted earlier about the joys of a turkey vulture eating one's corpse.) The retreat from sentimentality may lead an author to abandon romance as well. Krutch rejects sentimentality but views romance as a necessary antidote to the coldly scientific perspective. He "...doubts that even the scientist...can realize full human potentials if he is without wonder, or love, or a sense of beauty; if he looks on the nature of which he is a part with the cold eye of an outsider."[48] Leopold sees sentimentality as an immature form of romance, repugnant only if one's aesthetic development ends there.

> Our ability to perceive quality in nature begins, as in art, with the pretty. It expands through successive stages of the beautiful to values

[46] *Ibid.*, p. 140.
[47] *Ibid.*, p. 53.
[48] Krutch, *Best Nature Writing*, p. 13.

as yet uncaptured by language. The quality of [wilderness] lies, I
think, in this higher gamut. . .[49]

Of the three purists, Abbey devotes the most attention to the
role of romance, being torn between his rational convictions and
romantic emotions. Intellectually, Abbey believes that

> . . .the desert has no heart, that it presents a riddle which has no
> answer, and that the riddle itself is an illusion created by some limita-
> tion or exaggeration of the displaced human consciousness.
>
> This at least is what I tell myself when I fix my attention on what
> is rational, sensible, and realistic, believing that I have at last overcome
> that gallant infirmity of the soul called romance—that illness, that
> disease. . .[50]

Reluctantly Abbey concludes that ". . .the romantic view, while
not the whole of the truth, is a necessary part of the whole
truth."[51]

Romantic Primitivism *vs*. Peaceful Co-existence of Wilderness and Civilization

To some purists, wilderness and civilization seem antithetical:
in wilderness nature rules and man is absent or very subdued, but
in civilization man controls nature. If wilderness and civilization
are irreconcilable, it follows that to embrace one is to reject the
other. The romantic primitivists of the eighteenth and early
nineteenth centuries made a philosophical choice for wilderness.
Remnants of romantic primitivism sometimes identified with the
wilderness ethic bring additional confusion to the problem of
establishing a correct perception. Nature writers are concerned
with two aspects of romantic primitivism, the effect of each
environment on the personality and the practical economic relationship between wilderness and civilization.

The romantic primitivists of the Enlightenment believed that
primitive man in the wilderness developed a naturally noble personality, whereas civilized urban man became corrupt. (The extent to which this philosophical position was a stance for social
criticism cannot be evaluated here.) In contrast, the physiocrats
writing during the same period viewed nature as the Middle
Landscape, a scene of order and prosperity peopled by Jeffer-
son's yeoman farmers. Although the romantic primitivists and

---

[49] Leopold, *Sand County Sketches,* p. 96.
[50] Abbey, *Desert Solitaire,* p. 273.
[51] *Ibid.,* pp. 189-190.

the physiocrats agreed that virtue is foreign to the city, the farm and the wilderness were viewed as mutually exclusive ideals. In many parts of the American West, climate and terrain prevent the development of the type of middle landscape which exists in Europe and the Eastern United States. An eye accustomed to landscapes east of the hundredth meridian perceives the West as half-settled, more like the wilderness than the countryside. Accordingly, two distinct lines of thought intertwined to produce the Cowboy, a composite of the Noble Savage and the Honest Farmer. The shared element of non-urban virtue remained strong. Owen Wister's *The Virginian* is the classic statement of this composite of ideal personalities. If the Western rural resident is more noble than his urban counterpart, then by definition he should be more sensitive to the appeal of wilderness. Unfortunately, the experience of nineteenth century romantics with actual frontiersmen demonstrated that sensitivity was not one of the pioneer's strong suits, but the ideal of non-urban virtue was too appealing to be rejected for lack of factual support.[52]

Historically, the impulse for wilderness preservation has come from the upper middle classes of the Eastern Seaboard and San Francisco, whereas rural Western residents have tended to be more development-minded. For those who make their living from the land, development is a goal and a necessity. Rural residents near potential National Park or Wilderness Area sites have tended to perceive the reservation of parkland as a threat to their livelihood. Arizona cattlemen's fears of a reduction in their grazing privileges prevented the development of a state park system for many years.[53] Since World War II, the spread of social camping and middle-class resorts has caused a modification of this attitude, for social campers are a source of dollars to rural areas. Legally reserved Wilderness Areas are another matter, because relatively few people visit them and those who do prefer solitary environmental encounters to resort pleasures.

As we have seen in Chapter One, purists tend to be highly educated city dwellers rather than Noble Savages or Honest Countrymen. This paradox seems to reduce the validity of the

[52] Nash, *Call of the Wild,* p. 231.
[53] Marion Clawson and Burnell Held, *The Federal Lands: Their Use and Management.* Baltimore: The Johns Hopkins University Press, for Resources for the Future, Inc., 1957, p. 141.

entire wilderness ethic: if the people who live near wilderness are unappreciative, perhaps the wilderness ethic has no special merit. Perhaps the wilderness ethic is only an aesthete's pose? These questions have long been an embarrassment to the community of purists.

If we reject the premise that wilderness is the antithesis of civilization, difficulties caused by remnants of romantic primitivism disappear. Accordingly, nature writers since Thoreau have attempted to build the case that wilderness and civilization are really complementary rather than opposed. Through "contrast value"[54] and the reminder that man is dependent on nature, wilderness is thought to give definition and meaning to the human enterprise.[55] Thoreau believed that the balanced interplay between wilderness and civilization enriched human perception, and that the experience of alternating between the two poles helped develop a noble personality. If alternation was not possible, Thoreau suggested a permanent residence in partially cultivated country.[56] Abbey echoes Thoreau's point in his statement that the traditional Mormon towns of Utah achieved an ideal society, where men lived in harmony by carving out a very small middle landscape from the surrounding wilderness[57] (although Abbey neglects to mention whether this harmony was a product of the nineteenth century Mormon's technological limitations or of his aesthetic appreciation of nature).

Leopold's land ethic helps reconcile wilderness and civilization by defining the ability to appreciate wilderness as the herald of man's advance to a higher plane of civilization. Krutch agrees that wilderness appreciation is one of the marks of a truly civilized, cultivated man. As Krutch says

> . . .it is a return to nature which is most rewarding, after having spent some time in the city to acquire a civilized outlook.[58]

If wilderness appreciation is one of the graces of a civilized person, then all who fail to appreciate must be uncivilized. On occasion, the Sierra Club tends to lapse into this type of self-righteous reasoning.

---

[54] Leopold, *Sand County Sketches,* p. 179.
[55] *Ibid.,* p. 200.
[56] Nash, *Call of the Wild,* p. 92.
[57] Abbey, *Desert Solitaire,* p. 48.
[58] Krutch, *More Lives Than One,* pp. 312-313.

Although wilderness and civilization can be reconciled on an intellectual plane, the often-noted conflict between wilderness preservation and economic growth remains serious. The exploitation of some natural resources is a necessary condition for the existence of civilization, which in turn is a necessary condition for the development of the wilderness ethic. All three nature writers excoriate economic growth as self-defeating in the long run, and as a destroyer of civilized values. Abbey fears that

> . . .there is a cloud on my horizon. A small dark cloud no bigger than my hand. Its name is Progress.[59]

Abbey attempted to resolve the difficulty by distinguishing between civilization as a set of values and culture as a set of rather unattractive artifacts. Despite his tone of self-mockery, Abbey took the distinction seriously:

> Civilization is Jesus turning water into wine; culture is Christ walking on the waves. . . .
> Civilization is mutual aid and self-defense; culture is the judge, the lawbook, and the forces of Law and Order. . . .
> Civilization is Sartre; culture, Cocteau. . . .
> Civilization is the wild river; culture 592,000 tons of cement.[60]

Although this argument is a neat semantic side-step, it fails to resolve the conflict between wilderness preservation and economic growth.

Aldo Leopold believed that the conflict between wilderness preservation and economic growth was a consequence of failure to impose adequate ethical restraints on growth; the two goals were not inherently incompatible to him. Of course, if one assumes that application of the land ethic would foster "good" land use, and if wilderness preservation is defined as "good", then by definition the land ethic would encourage wilderness preservation. Abbey's and Leopold's semantic arguments intellectually reconcile wilderness and civilization but as long as economic growth is the basis of civilization, the relationship will in practice remain uneasy.

VERBAL IMAGES OF AN INDEPENDENT AND SELF-JUSTIFIED NATURAL WORLD

Purist nature writers attempt to build verbal images of an

---

[59] Abbey, *Desert Solitaire*, p. 48.
[60] *Ibid.*, pp. 276-277.

independent and self-justified natural world. The wilderness ethic recognizes nature as a rightful object of religious contemplation and ethical behavior, with wilderness itself as a symbol for the sacred power manifest in all creation. When an ethical relationship is formed between man and man, the two become equal in a special sense. They regard each other as fully human and worthy of consideration, rather than oneself (human) and the other (it). The wilderness ethic brings this special type of equality to the relationship between man and nature. Although man must use natural resources to live, nature is more than a cornucopia of resources. Because the whole planet is sacred space, it is self-justified, good in itself regardless of man's attitudes or uses. Wilderness serves as a reminder of the perfection and sacred character of nature. In this sense nature is independent of man even though man may be the ecological dominant.

The purist theorizes that the natural world is independent and self-justified, but the relationship between wilderness and civilization remains difficult. The crux of the problem is that the utilization of natural resources is a necessary condition for the existence of civilization, but resource utilization often involves the destruction of wilderness. At the same time, civilization is necessary for the development of wilderness appreciation. The purist is trapped in the practical reality of livelihood, which often leads him to sin against geopiety. The difficulty appears in concentrated form in the person of the prosperous city-dwelling purist.

Nature writers attempt to establish canons of "correct" perception; that is, perception fully consistent with the wilderness ethic. The essence of proper perception is the question: "In what sense is it valid to seek moral guidance from natural history, biological sciences, and landscape appreciation?" On the crude level of the pathetic fallacy, nature is personified to reflect the preoccupations of the subject. The result is often sentimental moralizing, as in turn-of-the-century "Christian ornithology." On a higher level, Krutch believed in a continuity of mood from nature to man, where both share the same underlying reality of creation through God's love. Continuity of mood differs from the sentimentality of the pathetic fallacy because it implies an equality of man and nature which sentimentality only condescends to accept. Leopold tied his version of continuity to the physical and biological facts of nature. To him, the land ethic was a highly evolved form of symbiosis, bringing useful results and spiritual benefits through proper practice. Krutch and Leopold both believed that religious insight may be stimulated by an intense awareness of nature. In this respect they wrote within the Christian transcendentalist tradition, with its romantic attitude of trust and faith in a benevolent sacred power. This attitude is a precondition for the development of proper perception, because romance implies a willingness to be swept away toward something greater than oneself.

Abbey's bleak vision and dark, rebellious mood reflects a main current in postwar letters. He believes that the landscape is devoid of moral significance and that the attempt to find it is merely another form of human vanity. Paradoxically, the realization of this fact helps one to break through to a higher form of perception. The independence and self-justification of nature is very important to Abbey; accordingly, any use of wilderness as a source of religious insight is a step backward toward the old roles of man the owner, nature the resource. Abbey's nature resembles the Jehovah of the Old Testament. Jehovah is his own justification and is often indifferent to man. At the same time Abbey does not reject the man-nature continuum altogether, because he has faith in the life-force which animates both him and the non-human world.

Despite the numerous difficulties, contradictions, and paradoxes within the wilderness ethic, it retains enough unity to function as an ideology. The wilderness ethic boils down to humility. Leopold said it best:

> The shallow-minded modern who has lost his rootage in the land assumes that he has already discovered what is important; it is such who prate of empires, political or economic, that will last a thousand years. . . .all history consists of successive excursions from a single starting-point, to which man returns again and again to organize yet another search for a durable scale of values. . . [which is] . . .why the raw wilderness gives definition and meaning to the human enterprise.[61]

VISUAL IMAGES: PURIST LANDSCAPE PHOTOGRAPHY

Purist landscape photography forms a special school of landscape art, distinguished by its attempt to capture wilderness as it

---

[61] Leopold, *Sand County Sketches,* p. 200.

appears to a mind in the midst of a transcendent experience. The folios of landscape photography published as the Sierra Club's Exhibit Format Series and Landforms Series represent an extraordinary visual statement of a state of mind and a system of belief. Just as heat and pressure reduced an ancient morass of rotten ferns and dinosaur bones to the carbon essence of a diamond, so purist photography compresses the somewhat inconsistent ideas of the wilderness ethic into "significant form." The contradictions remain, but they are lost in the photograph's dazzling visual impact.

Interdependence of Verbal and Visual Images

Purist photography resembles nature writing in its need to walk the tightrope over the pathetic fallacy and in its need to establish points of contact between science and art. The sentimental anthropomorphism of some nature writing finds its counterpart in banal landscape art, where the lazy or uninterested eye is jerked into responsiveness by visual storytelling or by an unusually vivid contrast of color or tone.[62] Postcard sunsets do not require delicacy of perception in the photographer or in his audience. Purist photographers resemble nature writers in their attempt to escape the pathetic fallacy by paying close attention to the facts of nature. Unfortunately, the facts of nature revealed by twentieth century science are both too large and too small for the imagination.[63] It is difficult for the layman or the artist to reconcile imaginatively curved space with mutating viruses.[64] The visual language inherited from nineteenth-century European landscape painting can express part of what the purist feels, but not what he knows. Part of the purist photographer's visual problem is to suggest the ecological unity behind the variety and dynamism of nature.

A work of art must be based on a dominating idea which is conveyed by a powerful sensual impression. In the case of purist landscape photography, the idea is the immanence of sacred power in nature. The test of an artist is his ability to carry an idea through by enriching and expanding the viewer's perception,

[62] Kenneth Clark, *Landscape Into Art*. London: John Murray, Ltd., 1949, p. 87.
[63] *Ibid.*, p. 141.
[64] Gyorgy Kepes, *Education of Vision*. New York: George Braziller, Inc., 1965; and *The New Landscape in Art and Science*. Chicago: Paul Theobald and Company, 1956.

without allowing the viewer to be seduced by superficially exciting incidents. How is this done? Kenneth Clark believes that

> Facts become art through love, which unifies them and lifts them to a
> higher plane of reality; and, in landscape, this all-embracing love is
> expressed by light.[65]

John Muir's name for the Sierra Nevada was "the Range of
Light," and his writings are crowded with descriptions of the
many variations of mountain light, its effect upon earthly and
heavenly objects, and its power in influencing his own moods. As
Muir said:

> I know not a single word fine enough for Light. Its currents pour, but
> it is a heavy material word not applicable to holy, bodiless, inaudible
> floods of Light.[66]

Muir attempted to do the same thing with prose as a landscape
artist does with paint, or a purist photographer does with film.
Outdoor photography limits an artist's options much more than
studio photography or painting. He cannot rearrange scenes for
greater visual impact. The success of his composition depends
largely on finding the right position for his camera and waiting
for the cooperation of weather and sunlight. The outdoor
photographer achieves some measure of control over the modula-
tions of light in the process of developing and printing his picture, but in the field he must wait and be ready for the special
moment. Since a landscape photographer cannot move mountains, he must suggest ideas with the light and shadow supplied
by nature.

Ansel Adams and Eliot Porter

The American tradition of landscape photography was formed
by the photographer-explorers of the late nineteenth century
West, such as O'Sullivan and W. H. Jackson. Like their counterpart in prose, John Wesley Powell, these photographers were part
scientist, part reporter, and part artist. Their purpose was to
explore, record, and understand the natural site. Today, American landscape photographers can be divided into two groups.

---

[65] Clark, *Landscape Into Art,* p. 16.
[66] John Muir, cited by Daniel Weber, *John Muir: The Function of Wilderness in an Industrial Society.* Unpublished Ph.D. dissertation, University of Minnesota, 1964, p. 123.

"Recorders," such as Eliot Porter, are closer to the nineteenth century tradition; "interpreters," such as Ansel Adams, are more personal and evocative in style.[67] Porter's work is characterized by a simple sensual delight in nature and by his empathy for the explorer's sense of anticipation. Adams' group attempts to charge a scene with special meaning without losing sight of the original object. Their work is suggestive, like much other modern art; one critic says that Adams photographs seem charged with the effects of psychology and psychoanalysis.[68]

Adams began his career in the 1920's, so much of his work is in black and white. Even his later color photographs are characterized by dramatic contrasts of light and shadow and by the sculptural quality he brings to rock. Adams likes contrasts which suggest unity; the soft, milky cloud mirrors the shape of a granite peak, fresh young grass surrounds a charred tree trunk, frost covers a stump and a leaf alike. Details are often contrasted with a panorama to show unity of form. Very few of his landscape photographs include people or human artifacts. When they are shown, people and buildings are dwarfed by huge clouds or almost lost in great distances, underscoring man's insignificance in relation to nature. Man-made artifacts in landscapes seem to attract Adams' approval only if they are sufficiently old, rough, weathered, massive, or primitive. The pueblos of Taos seem to belong in Adams' landscape, as do the weathered picket fences of the Napa Valley. Ruskin's belief that old, handmade objects are inherently more valid and authentic than modern machine-tooled creations is accepted as an article of faith not only by purist photographers, but by a whole school of contemporary taste. Adams' work exudes a sense of confidence in the power of correct perception. As his biographer Nancy Newhall says:

> The spectres of originality or of stereotype do not bother Adams. He approaches the weariest subject of the postcard makers as if only the wind had passed that way before. He knows his power. He knows he can make the commonplace into what only poetry and perhaps religion can explain.[69]

The most remarkable characteristic of Adams' style is the sense of Power in his landscapes. Trees, cliffs, and pueblo walls seem to

---

[67] Minor White, "The Photographer and the American Landscape," *Aperture*, Vol. 11, No. 2, February 1964, pp. 52-55.

[68] *Ibid.*

[69] Newhall, *Ansel Adams*, p. 18.

spring up out of the earth of their own accord. Clouds roll and boil with fearsome energy.

The landscape photography exhibit at the Museum of Modern Art in the autumn of 1963 included much of Adams' best work and caused a good deal of critical interest. Michael Gregory commented in *Aperture* that Adams' work attempts to create a union of opposites.

> . . .the irreconcilable opposition of forces *is* reconciled, tamed by the form itself—the shape of a cloud reflects the shape of a jagged peak. . .delicate tracery of oak branches and immense slabs of granite are mantled equally, without distinction, by an enshrouding snow-mist. Distinctions between "this" and "that," between "here" and "there" are resolved into a single *thus* which unifies the manifold aspects of the image.[70]

Minor White, also writing in *Aperture,* senses the numinous in Adams' photography:

> "Understanding" of nature is another dimension than love of nature, or a delight or terror in Nature's spawning and spurning of mankind all at once. At least I prefer to use the word "understanding" to give a handle to the Ansel Adams photographs. When nature is seen openly and objectively another force is occasionally glimpsed that is brilliant, clear, terrifying, compelling, brutal, magnificent, awesome, and anti-human. The Adams prints and images through their light and brilliant clarity suggest. . .the moment or two of Outsight in which Nature is understood. It is not a comfortable experience. It is joyous. Adams goes "through" to meaning beyond what is seen and those who are capable of an almost equal Outsight can penetrate beyond the surfaces. *Things for what they are* in the Adams images at times transcends both subject and manner. . .[71]

Adams' photography is remarkably close to Abbey's prose in its attitude toward nature: both are interested in the facts beyond the facts of nature. Both are somewhat uncomfortable about the inescapably spiritual content of their work. In 1925 Adams wrote

> . . .if I choose to photograph a rock, I must present a rock. . .the print must augment and enlarge the experience of a rock. . .stress tone and texture. . .yet never, under any circumstances, "dramatize" the rock, nor suggest emotional, or symbolic connotations other than what is obviously associated with the rock.[72]

What is "obviously" associated with a rock? The rocks in Adams'

[70] Michael Gregory, "Ansel Adams: The Philosophy of Light," *Aperture,* Vol. 11, No. 2, February 1964, pp. 49-51.
[71] White, "Photographer and American Landscape," p. 53.
[72] Letter fragment by Ansel Adams, no date. Cited in Newhall, *Ansel Adams,* p. 68.

photographs are quite different from the ones we experience every day, although they are clearly and recognizably themselves. Perhaps Adams was in tune with the 1920's vehement rejection of Victorian sentimentality, and attempted to refrain from the manipulation of conventional emotions by the use of conventional dramatic effects. He preferred to bring out the rock's own essence; however, in Adams' vision even a rock contains substantial portions of drama, emotion, and meaning.

Porter's vision is closer to the documentary landscape photographers of the late nineteenth century West. Porter's is any moment or the typical moment, not the special moment of Adams.[73] His photographs are full of the explorer's anticipation: what will I find over the next hill—a fantastic cactus, a rare bird, an unnamed bay? He departs from the nineteenth century tradition in his use of color and close-up detail. Brilliant color is the most striking element of Porter's style. He has much less sense of scale than Adams, and his outline and clarity of form are comparatively weak. He is less austere and disciplined, not at all hesitant to let his photographs sparkle. Porter's themes stress the vitality and persistence of life. He leans toward subjects such as roots emerging from cracks in rock, or a glitteringly green pool of algae-covered water in a rock depression. Porter photographs details more often than Adams, since details tend to provide sharp color contrasts and limit the area portrayed. Both photographers seem to disapprove of too much human influence in the landscape, although primitive or native objects are exceptions to the rule. Porter's photographs of ruined churches in Baja California have the same native quality as Adams' pueblos. Most important, the two photographers' work has an inescapably spiritual quality. According to one critic,

> One feels that the earth usurped Porter's vision and that Porter was willing to let it. . .the images make us envy Porter's contact with "moments of spirit," of breath and breathing. One of the meanings of "inspiration" is the breath of spirit warming the inner man. . .[74]

Sources of Style in Purist Photography

Purist photography is based on the heritage of landscape painting. It is relatively easy to thumb through a folio of purist prints

[73] John Upton, "Review of Two Books of Photos by Eliot Porter," *Aperture*, Vol. 11, No. 2, February 1964, pp. 82-83.
[74] *Ibid.*

and categorize each photograph in turn as "romantic," "modern," or "Chinese." Inherited styles are not yet completely reworked into a new purist style, although occasionally one sees individual photographs which have solved this problem.

Kenneth Clark suggests that four types of landscape painting exist within the Western tradition. The *landscape of symbols* was typical of medieval art. The representation of objects as themselves was not considered worthwhile; instead, certain objects were used symbolically to remind the viewer of Christian ideals. Many symbol-objects are not even recognizable to the modern eye: to us, they are abstract art. Later this rich symbolic vocabulary evolved into an art of decoration, characterized by a procession of attractive, two-dimensional, individually-seen symbol-objects.[75] The *landscape of fact* is characteristic of later painters such as Rembrandt. Light is used to unify the painting and to give it a sense of three-dimensional space. The painter's curiosity about the precise character of a place stimulated him to impassioned observation. Everything had to be recorded, from a humble detail to a grand perspective.[76] Rembrandt loved the facts of landscape, but observation is only the raw material for art. He created an imaginary world: vast, more dramatic, and more fraught with associations than what we can perceive for ourselves.[77] A landscape of fact is charged with meaning and emotion conveyed by the play of light, but the details within it do not have individual symbolic meaning. Purist photography appears to borrow many of its techniques from the landscape of fact.

The *landscape of fantasy* was an urban phenomenon of fifteenth century northern Europe. Nature had been tamed enough for the city dweller to brood on its remaining mysterious and unsubdued qualities without real fear. Nature could be used to excite a pleasing horror, much the way modern vampire movies play on the remnant of our superstitions. The landscape of fantasy bears a striking resemblance to modern expressionism, with its use of disturbing shapes and symbols. It is a forest art: dark, twisting, overwhelmingly alive, and highlighted for dramatic effect by fire and night.[78] The landscape of fantasy

[75] Clark, *Landscape Into Art*, pp. 19-31.
[76] *Ibid.*, p. 31.
[77] *Ibid.*, p. 36.
[78] *Ibid.*, p. 54.

indulges a "hard" primitivism; *ideal landscapes* represent a softer version of a garden world in a Golden Age. Ideal landscapes have a nostalgic and melancholy spirit, using classical composition to evoke a better world, now long past. Nature is tastefully groomed to meet human expectations.[79] Purist photography is closer to the landscape of fantasy. Jagged rocks, sun-bleached dead trees, rough surfaces, and boiling thunderclouds suggest a similar expressionist temperament. Ideal landscapes are more likely to be seen in the bucolic scenes favored by photographers with the Soil Conservation Service or the Army Corps of Engineers.

Landscapes of fact and fantasy give less emphasis to man's control of nature than do symbolic and ideal landscapes. A landscape of fact is beautiful for itself and as it is, regardless of human activities. Landscapes of fantasy are deliberately painted to seem slightly threatening and alien to man. Symbolic and ideal landscapes appreciate nature from a strictly human perspective. There is no hesitation to rearrange and improve nature to make it conform to canons of civilized taste. Purist photographers seem to find the techniques of landscapes of fact and fantasy somewhat more consistent with the wilderness ethic.

The purist photographer uses many visual devices from the European tradition of landscape painting, but Chinese and Japanese influences are equally important. Many photographs are so strikingly Chinese in appearance that they seem like deliberate experiments in imitation. This imitation is more than a question of fashion: Far Eastern painting may constitute the tradition of landscape art closest to the purist's vision. Michael Gregory compares Adams' vision to that of the Chinese landscape painter of the Sung Dynasty, Kuo Hsi. According to Gregory, for both artists the rendering of detail has more than strictly aesthetic significance. Trees, rocks, and mountains are made to stand for vast equivalents which are beyond ordinary speech and thought.[80] This is somewhat different from the symbolic landscape of the medieval West, where objects were stylized to the point of being almost unrecognizable to the contemporary eye. Adams and Kuo Hsi depict detail realistically, but it is what is not depicted that is most meaningful.

[79] *Ibid.*, p. 60.
[80] Gregory, "Ansel Adams," p. 50.

> What is perhaps the fundamental tenet of art (now almost completely forgotten in the West) is that reality lies outside the bounds of our consciousness, that reality is at once wider and incredibly more specific than our ideas about it can ever be.[81]

Chinese landscape painting of the T'ang and Sung Dynasties attempted to portray the sacred power immanent in nature. Sacred power itself cannot be painted, only its manifestations and their awesome, mysterious moods. Empty areas of a Chinese painting define what is painted and *vice versa,* suggesting the role of sacred power in our ordinary world.

> [In Chinese painting]. . .it has almost become a special art to paint empty space, to make it palpable, and to develop variations on this singular theme. Not only are there pictures on which "almost nothing" is painted, not only is it an essential feature of their style to make the strongest impression with the fewest strokes and the scantiest means, but there are very many pictures—especially those which are connected with contemplation—which impress the observer with the feeling that the void itself is depicted as a subject, is indeed the main subject of the painting.[82]

Chinese landscape painters would agree with nineteenth century American transcendentalists that to know nature more intimately is to come closer to an understanding of the sacred power immanent in nature. Chinese painters approached their goal with intuition and aesthetics; the American thinkers attempted the same thing with intuition and science. In the Chinese tradition, an encounter with nature is both psychic and intensely visual. Philosophers and poets wandered in the mountains in a joyful search for intimate and intuitive contact with sacred power through the medium of nature. Visual and psychic experiences were inextricably interwoven: bare rock and green foliage, heat and cold, light and shadow, sound and silence, high peaks contrasted against luscious, curving valleys. Landscapes suggested the relationship of opposites, *yin* and *yang,* through which the order of the universe might be understood.[83] Clearly, this mood is very similar to that of the purist photographer's.

The wilderness ethic places great value on an escape from cities into the purity of the wilderness. Chinese officials trained in

[81] *Ibid.,* pp. 68-69.
[82] Michael Sullivan, *The Birth of Landscape Painting in China.* Berkeley: University of California Press, 1962, p. 163.
[83] Arthur Waley, *An Introduction to the Study of Chinese Painting.* New York: Grove Press, Inc., 1923, p. 24.

Confucian concepts of political science and administration often sought relief from the din and bustle of government service in temporary retirement to the mountains. Taoism provided intellectual relief: it is an asocial philosophy associated in the Chinese tradition with escape to the mountains for solitary contemplation. Mountains and torrents were valued as means of escape into the reality of the Tao, as emblems of a world unspoiled by man's scheming and striving. This nostalgic desire for escape to a better world of nature colored Chinese landscape painting. It was not the plastic or purely visual side of landscape that inspired Chinese painters, but rather the mood and spiritual content of the scene.[84]

Numinous encounters with nature require symbols which are both abstract and visual. Symbolism hints at eternal, general truths while portraying forms which may be apprehended and recognized for what they are.

In *hsiang* symbolism, Chinese landscape painters developed an elaborate visual language, by which different combinations of symbols were used to express subtle meanings.[85] Purist photography has not yet evolved a language of symbols remotely comparable to the *hsiang* system. It seems very close to the Chinese tradition in spirit and intent, but at present cross-cultural influences appear to be restricted to characteristics of style.

The spare elegance of Chinese landscape painting and Japanese Zen taste resemble the contemporary Western taste for cool, formal design: "less is more." Strong, sculptural shapes seem to appeal to purist photographers for their "modern" quality. Contemporary Western taste also admires primitive art, which is formal but not necessarily cool; accordingly, purist photographers treat pueblos and ruined stone churches as assets to the wilderness landscape. The taste for formal primitivism is curiously mixed with remnants of John Ruskin's romanticism, and with the ideological position that nature and noble savages are better than modern technological man.

Purist photography is eclectic, its visual imagery inspired by European landscapes of fact and fantasy, by Chinese painting, and by modern formalism/primitivism. Borrowed styles do not yet appear to be fused into a uniquely purist style, but the purist

[84] *Ibid.*, pp. 138-139.
[85] Sullivan, *Birth of Landscape Painting*, pp. 5-6.

photographer's attempt to portray sacred power in nature is the theme which unifies his experiments.

THE EDUCATION OF VISION: VISUAL IMAGES AND PUBLIC OPINION

Like any other aspect of our inner lives, the wilderness experience is incoherent until we give it form. Illuminating personal contact with symbols of feeling helps us to achieve the intellectual and emotional order which integrates events into experience.[86] Purist photography provides the visual image which helps to refine and to train the viewer's perception. Purists learn elements of a "correct" mode of perception consistent with the wilderness ethic from photographs where every detail contributes to a powerful sensual impression and to a dominating idea. Purist nature writers and landscape photographers appear to have confidence in the power of this "education of vision" to transform the perception of their audiences, and perhaps to recruit new members to the community of purists. Verbal and visual images can be used to achieve political goals if they are sufficiently powerful to influence public opinion. The purist's inward action requires verbal and visual images to give form to his wilderness experiences; the same images become central to outward action when they are used as propaganda in political struggles over wilderness preservation. Purist leaders have long recognized the political value of verbal and visual images; indeed, John Muir, the founder of the Sierra Club, is better remembered today as a nature writer than as a scientist or as a political activist. Purist leaders have attempted to use visual images to mold public opinion in two ways: by influencing facility design in the National Parks and by publishing folios of purist landscape photography.

National Parks or Wilderness Areas as Aesthetic Experiences

It has been said that life is bad art: our ordinary experiences with nature are not nearly as intense or as well-organized as purist photographers suggest they should be. If the viewer were able to step into a photograph, so to speak, he would experience wilderness "correctly." By 1934, Ansel Adams had arrived at the idea that National Parks should be treated as aesthetic wholes,

[86] Langer, *Feeling and Form*, pp. 401-402.

almost as a work of art or as a multi-media museum. Natural and man-made details should blend harmoniously, allowing the visitor to immerse himself in a perfectly articulated sensual and intellectual experience. Visitors would leave the park with improved perception, their attitudes molded in favor of wilderness preservation. According to Adams, public appreciation of wilderness depends on the image formed by the "presentation" of National Parks. "Presentation" is used here to mean aesthetic unity of all details, including advertisements, informational pamphlets, souvenirs, landscape architecture, and buildings.

> The quality of the National Parks themselves and the spirit and intention on which they were created predicates a high level of taste in their operation.
>
> . . .there is lacking a subtle and hard-to-define element: the awareness of detail. . .little things. . .break the vital thread of perfection; they destroy the mood, which after all, is the most precious factor in the relation of man to nature.[87]

Adams particularly disliked the souvenir curios sold in Yosemite in the 1930's, such as kewpie dolls and heart-shaped cushions with "Mother" embroidered on one side and "Souvenir of Yosemite" on the other. He and his wife Virginia attempted to introduce curios they felt were more in harmony with the spirit of Yosemite, such as Indian jewelry and hand-carved wooden animals. The venture was a commercial failure.[88]

Paul Shepard has devoted a great deal of interest to styles of landscape painting as models for the public conception of beauty in nature. According to Shepard, the various National Parks reflect an ongoing evolution in public taste, with "natural beauty" being continuously expanded and redefined to fit changing pictorial criteria. "Parklike parks" were established in the early years of the national parks movement. They correspond to the hereditary images of the ideal landscape as expressed in the English gentleman's park, with a lawn, scattered trees, and a view. Beyond the lawn is scenery, usually defined as blue water, conifers, and snow-capped peaks. Yosemite Valley, for example, was first valued for Nature's extraordinary success in meeting human pictorial standards. The wild, gentleman's park is a

---

[87] Ansel Adams, "The Aesthetic Factor in Relation to Presentation of the National Parks," unpublished essay fragment, c. 1936. Cited in Newhall, *Ansel Adams*, p. 117-120.

[88] Newhall, *Ansel Adams*, pp. 117-120.

curious juxtaposition of ideals but, nevertheless, served as an image to judge the suitability of proposed park sites. "Unparklike parks" do not correspond to inherited, cherished images, but they are coming to be valued by the public for other characteristics. The Sierra Club's fight to prevent a dam from being built in Dinosaur National Monument attracted such widespread support as to catch the water-development lobby by surprise. According to Shepard,

> What the conservationists apparently wished to save was a fragment of the earth's primeval wilderness big enough and genuine enough to influence the imagination, particularly the urban mind. A large part of the public accurately sensed and shared this objective, partly an expression of an impulse to hold on to an aspect of the environment that has always been real to humanity: the uninhabited place and the reality of wilderness and danger.[89]

As we have seen, purist pictorial criteria are rapidly evolving away from traditional pastoral images in favor of another code: any landscape is beautiful (and hence worthy of some sort of appreciation and preservation), so long as it is wild. Purist political leaders attempt to use this code's visual image to rally public opinion and to lead it toward acceptance of wilderness preservation programs. New purists and purist sympathizers need not be recruited only in National Parks; they can be reached at home by landscape photography used as propaganda.

The Exhibit Format Series

The propaganda value of purist photography lies partially in its ability to shape perception without threatening the viewer. A political pamphlet is propaganda of an obvious kind, but landscape photography is equally effective without being offensive. More important, photographers help to stimulate agreement on what wilderness ought to be like. If our goal is to see as the photographer sees, the composition of a picture can suggest what is "good" and "bad" in the landscape. David Brower was perfectly aware of the utility of purist photography as a perception training device and acknowledged Ansel Adams as one of the greatest influences on the Sierra Club's publishing effort.

> Each place has its own genius. Adams reminds us of what the genius of man can see, if he looks insistently enough, of the genius of

[89] Paul Shepard, *Man in the Landscape: A Historic View of the Aesthetics of Nature.* New York: Alfred A. Knopf, 1967, pp 265-266.

nature. . . .As a photographer of great places, he came quickly to dis-
cover what did not belong in those places. . . .He quickly learned to
single out the little and big things that eroded the mood.[90]

The propaganda value of purist photography was recognized
by Sierra Club leaders twenty-five years before the Club entered
its militant phase in the 1960's. In 1936, the Sierra Club sent
Ansel Adams to Washington to lobby on behalf of the proposed
King's Canyon National Park. "In this, as the Club knew, his
photographs would be more effective than a six-volume
report."[91] Adams' photographs were published in a folio titled
Sierra Nevada: The John Muir Trail, which proved an instant
success. When King's Canyon National Park was established in
1938, the Director of the National Park Service wrote to Adams:
"I realize that a silent but most effective weapon in the campaign
was your own work. . . .So long as that book is in existence it
will go to justifying the park."[92]

Ironically, in the 1930's Adams was accused by socially conscious photographers of being an irresponsible advocate of art for
art's sake. The other-worldly quality of his work was to some
critics old-fashioned and irrelevant in the struggle for a more
humane social order. Adams replied:

> My training has been introspective and intensely lonely. I have been
> trained with the dominating thought of art as something almost
> religious in nature. As I look back on it now, I realize a certain
> "unworldly" quality about [this] point of view. . . .For quite a few
> years, I have.been fully aware that something was missing. . .the "con-
> tact with life" you may call it. . .I distrust the power of Propaganda as
> Art, or the power of Art as Propaganda (in the obvious sense, of
> course). But I don't distrust the power of Propaganda as Propaganda.
> And more power to those who are working for the betterment of the
> social order.[93]

Around 1962, Nancy Newhall saw an exhibit of Eliot Porter's
work at the George Eastman House in Rochester, New York, and
brought it to the attention of David Brower, then Executive
Director of the Sierra Club. Brower decided to publish Porter's
exhibit in folio form to celebrate the Thoreau centenary. As the
wife of Beaumont Newhall (who was then photography curator

---

[90] David Brower, "Introduction," in Newhall, *Ansel Adams,* p. 7.
[91] Newhall, *Ansel Adams,* pp. 123-124.
[92] Letter of Arno B. Cammer to Ansel Adams, 1940. Cited in Newhall, *Ansel Adams,* p. 126.
[93] Ansel Adams, letter fragment, c. 1936. Cited in Newhall, *Ansel Adams,* p. 126.

of the Museum of Modern Art), active Sierra Club member, and the friend and later biographer of Ansel Adams, Mrs. Newhall was well qualified to set in motion the publishing ventures which did so much to attract nationwide attention to the Sierra Club. A $50,000 grant from Kenneth and Nancy Bechtel through the Belvedere Scientific Fund made publication possible.[94] The result was *In Wildness is the Preservation of the World*, with photographs by Eliot Porter, text from the collected works of Henry David Thoreau, and introduction by Joseph Wood Krutch. The venture was a critical and popular success, and won numerous awards for technical excellence and distinguished publishing.[95] *In Wildness is the Preservation of the World* was followed by *This is the American Earth* (photographs: Ansel Adams, text: Ansel Adams and Nancy Newhall) and *The Eloquent Light* (photographs: Ansel Adams, text: Nancy Newhall), and eventually by all the titles which comprise the Exhibit Format Series. The series has received widespread praise: one critic called *The Eloquent Light* "electrifying" in its effect on perception.[96]

Throughout the 1960's, Brower expanded and diversified the Club's publishing efforts to include posters, paperbacks, wall calendars, stationery, and motion picture shorts. He hoped to achieve a complex, coordinated network of wilderness preservation propaganda which would equal the effect of propaganda by development interests. Brower planned to create an international climate of public opinion favorable to wilderness preservation— his vision was no longer limited to North America—and he was investigating the possibility of television documentaries when the Sierra Club Board of Directors removed him from office.[97] Although Brower's publishing efforts were a critical, popular, and political success, the high level of bookmaking quality Brower demanded made the folios, posters, etc., expensive to produce and expensive to buy. By the late 1960's, Brower had $1 million tied up in inventory, amounting to half the Sierra Club's annual budget. Fearing bankruptcy, the Club's Board of Directors removed him from office.[98]

---

[94] *Publisher's Weekly*, "Sierra Club's Thoreau Book Marks Expanding Program," Vol. 182, October 1, 1962, pp. 78+.

[95] *Ibid.*

[96] R.A. Jones, "Fratricide in the Sierra Club," *Nation*, Vol. 208, May 5, 1969, pp. 567-570.

[97] *Ibid.*

[98] *Ibid.*

During Brower's tenure, Sierra Club publications were criticized from time to time for their exclusive concentration on wilderness. Although *This is the American Earth* included photographs of pastoral, settled landscapes, later folios tended to exclude human beings and human artifacts. In 1972, the Sierra Club's new Executive Director, Michael McCloskey, announced a new publishing effort called the Landform Series, beginning with a study of the Great Plains entitled *The Floor of the Sky*.[99] Unlike the Exhibit Format Series, which concentrated on particular places such as Glen Canyon or Glacier Bay, the Landform Series attempted to consider physiographic provinces, cultural regions, or groups of places with a dominant landform in common . (beaches, estuaries).[100] The Landform Series was planned to highlight what Ellen Churchill Semple called ". . .the life-giving connection between land and people;"[101] that is, to carry a conservation message as opposed to a wilderness preservation theme. This shift in emphasis is connected to a new ideological and political position within the community of purists, as will be explored later. According to McCloskey, the general purposes of the Landform Series were identical to those of the Exhibit Format Series: to make a profit for the Sierra Club's legal fund, to attract new members, and to convey the Club's message to the public.[102] Only the content of the message was to be changed. McCloskey supplemented the Landform Series with a series of books on environmental problems, both urban and rural, dominated by expository text rather than by photographs. Topics awaiting publication include studies of the pollution effects of power plants and waste disposal, transportation problems, urban wildlife, and the ecology of individual habitats.[103]

Not all daily events become intense personal experiences. Experience is not something which "just happens;" it is an act of intellectual and emotional organization which occurs when an individual understands the significance of an event in terms of

[99] *Publisher's Weekly*, "New Sierra Books to Feature People," Vol. 201, March 6, 1972, p. 49.
[100] *Ibid.*
[101] Ellen Churchill Semple, *Influences of Geographic Environment.* New York: H. Holt and Company, 1911, p. 1.
[102] *Publisher's Weekly*, "New Sierra Books," p. 49.
[103] *Publisher's Weekly*, "Sierra Club's Future Publishing Plans," Vol. 197, February 2, 1970, p. 68.

symbolic form. Wilderness imagery lends conceptual and emotional prominence to the wilderness ethic. A striking landscape description, a beautiful photograph, or a perfectly detailed National Park lend form to individual feeling, hence intensifying feeling by placing it in a common syntax by which it may be shared with others, contemplated in memory, or compared to other experiences. It is a truism that one's emotional and intellectual orientation toward events strongly influences eventual actions. Purist leaders recognize the impact of wilderness imagery on the organization of individual feelings and beliefs, and take care to disseminate this verbal and visual imagery throughout the community of purists and the wider public. This imagery solidifies the loyalty of the community of purists, increases the community's political effectiveness, and popularizes the wilderness ethic among the general public. The manner in which purists' outward action depends on the imagery derived from inward action must now be examined in order to identify the political implications of this imagery for wilderness preservation and for the environmental movement.

III

Object and Subject in Reciprocal Relation: Outward Action

THE WILDERNESS ETHIC, PERSONAL BEHAVIOR, AND POLITICS

O utward action may be considered as a set of logically related attempts to put the intellectual and emotional implications of the wilderness ethic into practice in the "real world." Purist personal behavior in wilderness is guided by a code derived from the wilderness ethic and its imagery; purist political pressure group activities attempt to make public and private land management practices consistent with wilderness values.

Purist personal behavior in wilderness and purist pressure group activities resemble one another in the sense that they function simultaneously as rituals of allegience to the community of purists and as successful methods to enjoy the wilderness and to preserve its character. The term "ritual" should not be interpreted as an empty or meaningless activity, for all cultures use ritual to involve members of a community in a common enterprise which focuses attention on their connectedness and joint interests. Ritual encourages conformity and joyful satisfaction in conformity by merging the individual with the group.[1] It is no accident that many purists participate in wilderness sports such as backpacking, ski mountaineering, and canoeing, for such activities can function simultaneously as enjoyable wilderness outings and as spiritual/aesthetic exercises which strengthen commitment to wilderness values. Purist leaders recognize the role of ritualized personal behavior in wilderness, and encourage fellow

[1] Murray Edelman, *The Symbolic Uses of Politics.* Urbana: University of Illinois Press, 1964, p. 16.

purists to participate in pressure-group-sponsored wilderness out-ings.

Group political behavior is the second aspect of outward action. Role-playing in conflict situations helps to create a group sense of identity, a function almost as important as achieving stated political goals. Murray Edelman believes that role-playing is socially-cued rather than empirically based,[2] suggesting that one chooses a role as an act of allegience to persons similar to oneself. Essentially, purist political action attempts to prevent landscape changes which conflict with the wilderness ethic by influencing public land management policies and by extending public authority over private land. Verbal and visual images of wilderness become political goals: purist political activity at-tempts to prevent real wilderness areas from changing in a man-ner inconsistent with the image, and attempt to make settled landscapes as much like the image as possible.

BEHAVIOR IN WILDERNESS

Purist Behavior: Minimizing Human Presence and Power

The wilderness ethic shapes purist behavior by lending "recre-ation" many of the qualities of a ritual of purification. Purists enjoy their wilderness outings, of course, but their pleasure is saturated with a higher seriousness. Since purist definitions of enjoyable wilderness sports are based on the axiom and corol-laries of the wilderness ethic, purist sports tend to minimize human presence and power. Purists act out their worshipful humility by temporarily surrendering modern conveniences—our means of mastery over nature—in favor of a few day's existence at a primitive level of technology. The backpack and the canoe are material expressions of the purist's inward action.

The purist's desire to be as unobtrusive as possible in the wilderness is summarized by the slogan, "Take only pictures, leave only footprints." Trash is anathema: Hendee found that purists agree that everyone is obliged to help clean up other

---

[2] Murray Edelman, *Politics as Symbolic Action: Mass Arousal and Quiescence.* Chicago: Markham Publishing Company, for the Institute for Research on Poverty, Monograph Series, 1971, p. 10

campers' litter.[3] Unpolluted campsites are a physical expression of respect for sacred space; litter is a desecration. The purist's code requires one to:

1) dig a sump hole for wash water
2) refrain from washing directly in lakes and streams
3) bury or pack out all non-combustible trash
4) refrain from "improving" a campsite with bough beds, etc.
5) restrict campfires to established firescars
6) speak critically to anyone breaking these rules[4]

Clean, uncluttered campsites contribute to the illusion that each purist is alone in nature. The opportunity for solitude is a very important element in the wilderness ethic; thus, evidence of other people is almost as destructive to the wilderness mood as actual crowding.

Human power is minimized by the surrender of motor vehicles at the edge of the wilderness. Purists dislike motorized recreational vehicles for many reasons. First, vehicles are thought to feed human egoism by allowing people to cruise the wilderness at will. In contrast, self-propelled travel is limited by the weather and by the weakness of the flesh. Second, automobiles and camper vehicles require roads, which are forbidden in wilderness by definition. Third, motorized recreational vehicles and outsiders go together in the purist's mind, since presumably those with inferior perception do not go to the trouble of penetrating wilderness by purist methods. Most important, motor vehicles are simply bad manners in sacred space. Says Abbey,

> We have agreed not to drive our automobiles into cathedrals, concert halls, art museums, legislative assemblies, private bedrooms, or other sanctums of our culture. We should treat our National Parks with the same deference, for they, too, are holy places. . . .We are finally learning that the forests and the mountains and the desert canyons are holier than our churches.[5]

Remoteness and difficulty of access are essential parts of the appeal of wilderness; both are destroyed by the intrusion of recreational vehicles. In discussing Glen Canyon Dam's effect in

[3] John C. Hendee *et al., Wilderness Users in the Pacific Northwest: Their Characteristics, Values, and Management Preferences.* U.S. Forest Service, Pacific Northwest Forest and Range Experiment Station, Research Paper PNW-61, p. 36.
[4] *Ibid.,* pp. 36-42.
[5] Edward Abbey, *Desert Solitaire: A Season in the Wilderness.* New York: Ballantine Books, Inc., 1971. p. 60.

opening formerly remote canyonlands to motorboat traffic, Abbey deals with remoteness as an element in the beauty of Rainbow Bridge.

> The new dam will improve things. If ever filled it will back water to within sight of the Bridge, transforming what was formerly an adventure into a routine motorboat excursion. Those who see it then will not understand that half the beauty of Rainbow Bridge lay in its remoteness. . .when this aspect is removed the Bridge will be no more than an isolated geological oddity, an extension of that museum-like diorama to which industrial tourism tends to reduce the natural world.[6]

The physical struggle of self-propelled wilderness travel heightens the purist's spiritual involvement. Accordingly, purists believe that easy access by recreational vehicle contributes to superficial perception of wilderness.

Robert Lucas feels that the superficial attitudes associated with motorized wilderness recreation are also associated with callousness toward the physical well-being of wilderness.

> I think someone should challenge irresponsible advertising of trail bikes, ATVs, and snowmobiles. Too many ads glorify conquering nature and ignore the damage done.
> For example, one ATV ad says, "Even two-to-three inch trees topple—just drive right through trees and brush." ATV and trail bike ads show wet meadows being ripped up, mud flying from wheels churning up trails, and slopes so steep they are frightening being mastered—and eroded. Impossible and even illegal images are presented, such as the "sportsman" seated on his trail cycle shooting a presumably deaf deer. . . .I do not see why public recreation officials need to feel obliged to somehow accommodate anything the engineers can concoct and the advertising men mis-represent.[7]

Purist publications increasingly stress the importance of proper behavior in wilderness. The rapid spread of the wilderness ethic in the past decade has created an army of wilderness users, whose perception and behavior lie halfway between the outsider's and the purist's. An obscure example illustrates the widespread concern of purists with proper behavior. Recreational Equipment, Incorporated is a cooperative mail-order sporting goods firm headquartered in Seattle, and has long been associated with the community of purists. R.E.I. catalogues now include an editorial page (printed on 100 percent recycled paper) which attempts to define the "new wilderness ethic." According to R.E.I.,

[6] *Ibid.*, p. 217.
[7] Robert C. Lucas, "Hikers and Other Trail Users," *Recreation Symposium Proceedings,* U.S. Forest Service, Northeast Forest Experiment Station, 1971, p. 120.

The situation in the back country now calls for everyone to do more than his or her part. This means packing out your own garbage *plus* any other litter you find. It also means speaking to anyone who treats the wilderness harshly. . . .We do not wish to discourage the use of the outdoors, but rather to instill a sense of caution in all who use the back country.[8]

R.E.I. believes that proper perception is the reward of hiking, backpacking, and other self-propelled sports. However, the editor reminds us sternly that ". . .no one has the right to these rewards unless he or she accepts personal responsibility for the preservation of our vanishing wildlands."[9] R.E.I. quotes Harvey Manning's *Backpacking One Step at a Time* for a summary of activities in harmony with the wilderness ethic.

Ecology. . .should be the hiker's passion, not merely to enrich his pleasure but so he may understand the functioning of individual ecosystems and how to fit into them as unobtrusively as possible. He should. . .gain a feel for the dynamic balance of a river, of a glacier, and how they carve valleys. And grow intimate with the trees and flowers, mosses and lichens, fungi and molds. . .And at night he should look out to the moon and stars and deeply comprehend this is the only Earth we ever will have.[10]

Case Study: The Lake Melakwa Cleanup

In midsummer of 1973, 120 R.E.I. members spent a day collecting and removing trash from the high country lakes in a Cascade Range Wilderness Area near Seattle. Assisted by the Forest Service, the State Department of Ecology, the Mayor of Seattle, and the Governor's son, the volunteers trudged as far as 14 1/2 miles to remove evidence of human presence from the wilderness. "The size of the parties was kept to approximately twenty each so as to minimize our personal impact on the fragile environment,"[11] the R.E.I. editor reported. Redundant fire pits were smoothed over, leaving only those in locations which "minimize ecological damage."[12] Old campsites within 100 feet of a lake or stream were destroyed and new ones established at a distance that would "limit man's influence on the water."[13]

[8] Jim Whittaker (ed.), "Lake Melakwa Clean-up Proves Successful," *Viewpoint*, Vol. 2, September 1973, Seattle: Recreational Equipment, Inc., pp. 21-24.
[9] *Ibid.*
[10] *Ibid.*
[11] *Ibid.*
[12] *Ibid.*
[13] *Ibid.*

Scuba divers packed in their weightbelts, wet suits, and tanks to clean litter off the lake bottoms.

> By 3:00 p.m., most of the garbage had been accumulated in plastic sacks and placed adjacent to the lake areas. At this point we all took a deep breath, loaded our packs up with as much of the debris as everyone could carry. . .and began our descent. . . .We had been offered helicopter assistance on the clean-up, but felt it was better to try to do the whole project on foot in hopes that our non-mechanical example would encourage other groups or individuals to sponsor clean-ups.
>
> By 6:30 p.m., we were on our way back to Seattle.[14]

Several interesting points emerge from this report. First, the volunteers used the term "ecologically damaging" interchangeably with "unaesthetic," underscoring the importance of Leopold's fusion of science with the wilderness ethic. Second, it would have been far more "practical" to remove the collected litter with helicopters rather than with backpacks, but the backpack method was perceived as morally preferable. This preference shows political insight, since the purpose of the Lake Melakwa clean-up was threefold: to remove the litter, to offer the opportunity for purists to reaffirm their allegience to the wilderness ethic through ritualized personal action, and to teach wilderness users outside the community of purists that proper behavior in wilderness minimizes human presence and power. Both volunteers and reporters understood the propaganda value of their efforts.

Purist Self-Images: Are Purists "Elitists?"

Purists are often accused of being "backpack snobs," an "aristocracy of the physically fit," who criticize the harmless pleasures of social campers as part of an effort to monopolize scarce recreational resources. This caricature dies hard because it contains an element of truth, like a good political cartoon. Although the community of purists finds the accusation of elitism a perpetual source of embarrassment, purists appear to feel that they possess a higher form of perception than outsiders. Abbey labels outsiders with the pejorative term "industrial tourists" and excoriates their supposed timidity, ignorance, and indifference to geopiety.[15] Leopold could not resist a sarcastic swipe:

---

[14] *Ibid.*
[15] Abbey, *Desert Solitaire*, pp. 45-69.

> Like ions shot from the sun, the weekenders radiate from the town, generating heat and friction as they go.[16]

In another mood, Leopold found the outsider's indifference to geopiety depressing. Discussing the activities of passengers on a bus trip across Illinois, Leopold said:

> The highway stretches like a taut tape across the corn, oats, and clover fields; the bus ticks off the opulent miles; the passengers talk and talk and talk. About what? About baseball, taxes, sons-in-law, movies, motors, and funerals, but never about the heaving groundswell of Illinois that washes the windows of the speeding bus. Illinois has no genesis, no history, no shoals or deeps, no tides of life and death. It is only the sea on which they sail to ports unknown.[17]

Purists respond to an idea of wilderness and to certain restricted pictorial criteria, whereas outsiders respond primarily to other people, secondarily to the visual cliché of scenery.

Abbey's opinion of the mass of mankind is clear: "I'm a humanist. I'd rather kill a *man* than a snake."[18] But Abbey is aware of the irony of the elitist pose. He describes a trail registration book at the mouth of a remote canyon: " 'Keep the tourists out' some fellow tourist from Salt Lake City has written. As fellow tourists we heartily agree."[19] Purists resent the outsider's presence in sacred space because his "inferior" mode of perception allows him to enjoy and inadvertently to desecrate wilderness. The Moslem removes his shoes at the door of the mosque, the purist parks his car at the trailhead, but the blundering tourist snaps flashbulbs in the cathedral and rides trailbikes in the woods.

On the other hand, purist leaders hope that education might elevate the outsider's perception and improve his manners. Every outsider is a potential purist. The folios of landscape photography published by the Sierra Club may be considered sophisticated forms of the missionary's pamphlet. David Brower reminded his interviewer of Billy Graham:

> Brower's crusade may be more effective than Graham's because present concern about the environment is sort of a delayed echo of what Brower has been saying for decades. . .he is. . .a visionary, an

---

[16] Aldo Leopold, *A Sand County Almanac and Sketches Here and There.* New York: Oxford University Press, 1969, p. 165.
[17] *Ibid.*, p. 119.
[18] Abbey, *Desert Solitaire*, p. 20.
[19] *Ibid*, p. 283.

emotionalist in an age of dangerous reason. [According to Brower, wilderness preservation should be]. . .an ethic and conscience in everything we do, whatever our field of endeavor.[20]

Outsiders may feel that this geopiety is both extreme and absurd. ". . .a man in an audience in Scarsdale once told Brower that to be consistent with his philosophy he should wear a skin and live in a cave."[21] Despite such devastating comments, the growth of the community of purists since World War II, the percolation of purist imagery into popular consciousness, and the passage of the Wilderness Act of 1964 have indicated some success in purist efforts to overcome the charge of elitism by broadening their base of popular support.

Professional Behavior: The Role of Wilderness Managers

Most wilderness managers are employees of the U. S. Forest Service. Their perception of wilderness tends to be colored by day-to-day management responsibilities. A public agency's reason for being is to translate the will of the people as stated by Congress into concrete reality, as directed by the Executive Branch. Typically, Congress sets broad policy goals in the legislation creating each public agency, usually modifying and updating these goals as the nation's needs change. Congressional directives may contain hidden contradictions, or the policy goal acceptable to the majority of the public may be anathema to a minority. In administering federal public lands, public agencies must attempt to resolve contradictions whenever necessary and appease minority groups whenever possible. When the use pressure on the public lands is low, incompatible land uses are able to coexist in separate sectors. When use pressure is high, managers must establish a priority ranking of incompatible land uses for each land segment. For every land use permitted by law except grazing, use pressure on the public lands has expanded at an increasing rate every year since World War II.[22]

The Wilderness Area system was created by Congress in recognition of the problems caused by increasing recreational use

---

[20] John McPhee, *Encounters with the Archdruid.* New York: Farrar, Straus and Giroux, 1971, p. 83.
[21] *Ibid.*, p. 95.
[22] Marion Clawson and Burnell Held, *The Federal Lands: Their Use and Management.* Baltimore: The Johns Hopkins University Press, for Resources for the Future, Inc., 1957, pp. 45-131.

pressure on the public lands. Prior to the Wilderness Act of 1964, social camping and purist recreation were not differentiated in law. Unofficially, however, certain parts of the National Forest system had long been administered as "primitive areas," with roads and economic uses being excluded. The Wilderness Act simply froze existing administrative practice. The first primitive area was established in 1924 in Gila National Forest of New Mexico, partially through the efforts of Aldo Leopold. Robert Marshall's influence in the Forest Service contributed to the establishment of 72 primitive areas by 1939.[23]

Although the Forest Service acted independently to preserve primitive areas, its first concern has been to provide natural resources for the nation. Wilderness may be viewed as a resource like any other, to be managed for recreation rather than for the timber harvest. The difference between wilderness recreation and social camping was recognized to a certain extent, or primitive areas would not have been established at all. At the same time, the Forest Service did not move as far in the direction of the wilderness ethic as purists thought it should. This mild disagreement was of little consequence prior to 1945, but gained importance with the post-war recreation boom. As Brower said, "...the early days were comfortable. Hikers and rangers and packers could get together to seek ways to extend their good times in the High Sierra...those were easy days when problems were neat."[24]

Prior to the passage of the Wilderness Act, Forest Service professionals tended to be somewhat skeptical about the idea of an official national wilderness preservation system. Wilderness Areas are undeveloped versions of National Parks, requiring a rigid and exclusive form of recreational land use which conflicts with the Forest Service policy of "multiple use." The duty of the Forest Service is to provide "multiple use management of natural resources for sustained yield to provide increasingly greater service to a growing nation."[25] The production of wood, water, wildlife, and minerals is supposed to coexist with recreation. Forest Service personnel assigned to Wilderness Areas must limit their ef-

[23] United States Forest Service, *National Forest Wildernesses and Primitive Areas.* Washington, D.C.: Government Printing Office, 1968.
[24] David Brower (ed.), *Wilderness: America's Living Heritage.* San Francisco: Sierra Club, 1961, p. vii.
[25] U.S. Forest Service, *National Forest Wildernesses.*

forts to the production of a specialized form of recreation. By training, Forest Service professionals have none of the purist's squeamishness about land use, realizing that their new duty of wilderness preservation requires the application of management technology.

Aldo Leopold gave a great deal of thought to the problem of wilderness mangement, long before it became a problem with a name. According to Leopold, the professional recreation manager is analogous to an opera producer. Both opera and recreation are aesthetic exercises which require hidden economic machinery to create and maintain facilities. As in opera, professionals make a living from the production of a mood or state of mind in an audience of connoisseurs.[26] Obvious stage machinery would conflict with the illusion of theater, therefore the curtains are manipulated quietly, out of sight of the audience. Professional land managers must protect wilderness by providing the facilities and regulations which are the necessary armor against destruction by use pressure, without management methods becoming obvious enough to destroy the wilderness mood. Above all, professionals must never lose sight of their main goal: ". . .to promote perception is the only truly creative part of recreational engineering."[27] Leopold believed that the rudimentary grades of outdoor recreation consumed their resource base, whereas the higher grades created their own satisfaction with no attrition of land or life. Therefore, the best way to prevent wilderness damage from overuse is to raise the perception of each recreationist, until he accepts the slogan "take only pictures, leave only footprints." Adams conceived of a National Park as an aesthetic whole, designed to foster proper perception through the structure and detail of its facilities. Leopold's conception of recreational land management was somewhat similar: "Recreational development is a job not of building roads into lovely country, but of building receptivity into the still unlovely human mind."[28] The manager's reward for the successful completion of this task is the subtle pleasure of "wild husbandry." Leopold regarded wildland management as a special type of farming, requiring a high order of taste, perception, and ethical restraint. Subtle as it is, wild hus-

---

[26] Leopold, *Sand County Sketches*, p. 167.
[27] *Ibid.*, p. 176.
[28] *Ibid.*, p. 184.

bandry violates the axiom of the wilderness ethic, because it manages and uses wilderness to satisfy human needs. The professional's opera-like stage management of wilderness can create public relations problems through its very success. Much of the conflict between purists and professionals stems from this disagreement.

One forester characterized the wilderness purist as ". . .a thoughtful, educated, sincere. . .individualist, although sometimes he is not as cognizant of the wilds as we professional people might desire."[29] Another warned that "fanatical wilderness cultists" are unsympathetic to any form of wilderness management because they do not understand that the adaptive and recuperative powers of the earth's biosphere preclude a static, "hands off" approach to wilderness management.[30] Hendee has high regard for the purist's personality and reservations about his understanding of the manager's problems.

> Wilderness purists are more perceptive of wilderness values and their opinions should receive added consideration. Wilderness management should not be as sensitive to the preferences of users whose activities do not depend exclusively on wilderness for their satisfaction. . . .It is vital for wilderness managers to be aware of differences in sentiment among different types of users so that the appropriate public can be informed as to the necessity of a policy before it is implemented.[31]

The purist is more attuned to the nuances of wilderness management than the ordinary outdoor recreationist, so wilderness managers are obliged to pay close attention to purist "critical reviews." Despite his sensitivity to wilderness aesthetics, the purist-as-critic may be unaware of the reasons behind certain backstage activities. He may look upon management tools such as helicopters and chain saws with a jaundiced eye. Sometimes, he may fear that professionals may tend to over-manage and to destroy wilderness in order to save it. Purists are most interested in the wilderness mood, and object to anything that theatens to break "the vital thread of perfection." For example, purists prefer route-marking signs to be made of wood rather than metal, although metal is more durable. Purists consider interpretive signs

---

[29] George A. Craig, "Foresters, Facts, and Philosophy in the Resource Policy Mix," *Journal of Forestry*, Vol. 64, October 1966, p. 664.
[30] F.B. Lamb, "Elements of Wilderness Management," *Journal of Forestry*, Vol. 71, September 1973, p. 588.
[31] Hendee *et al.*, *Wilderness Users*, p. 36.

a defacement, but they are happy to receive small, lightweight guidebooks to carry in their packs.[32] These and similar preferences add to the difficulty of the manager's job.

For the most part, managers and purists resemble one another in their perception of wilderness. Hendee and Harris found that managers anticipate purists' desires correctly two-thirds of the time. The professional's attitudes toward his clients reflect his vulnerable political position. Most professionals are exposed to user preferences only when someone complains; therefore, they are most aware of the points of disagreement between purists and social campers. Much of the manager's work is caused by problem users, which sometimes leads him to feel harassed by unreasonable and inconsistent demands. According to Hendee,

> A wilderness trip to many users is like a pilgrimage to a place viewed with near reverence. To managers such a trip may mean diversion from other pressing duties and responsibilities, and hard work to be performed under unduly difficult conditions. The point is that managers might easily take wilderness and its values for granted, or appear to do so. . .[33]

How can wilderness be managed to meet purist preferences if in providing the regulations and facilities necessary to protect it from use pressure by social campers, an almost impossible burden is placed on the professional manager? A favorite professional suggestion is that the root of the use pressure problem lies in urban environmental degradation: improved recreational facilities in the city would reduce the weekend exodus, presumably stemming the tide of wilderness visitors.[34] Dasmann takes a determinist position on this issue:

> If we build cities that are concrete deserts or inhabited only by rats and starlings, we will make a home only for rat-like people and colonial-roosting people of that kind who foul their environment.[35]

A second management suggestion is that wilderness areas should be made difficult to find and hard to use. Publicity lures visitors; therefore, an end to publicity would have obvious value in stabilizing use. Designating a place as a park or wilderness area

[32] *Ibid.*, p. 48.

[33] John C. Hendee and Robert W. Harris, "Foresters' Perception of Wilderness User Attitudes and Preferences." *Journal of Forestry,* Vol. 68, December 1970, p. 762.

[34] William R. Catton, Jr., "The Proposals as Viewed by a Sociologist," *Journal of Forestry,* Vol. 66, July 1968, p. 542.

[35] Raymond F. Dasmann, *A Different Kind of Country.* New York: The Macmillan Company, 1968, p. 178.

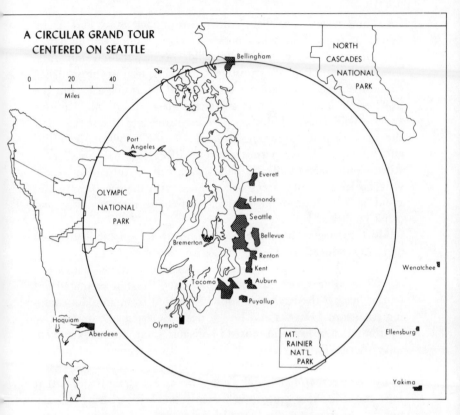

Figure 6   A Circular Grand Tour Centered on Seattle

with no other change causes an immediate increase in its use. Along the same lines, some managers argue that wilderness areas should be established in locations far from the tourist circuit. If the case of the National Parks is any guide, a park's attractiveness depends greatly on its proximity to cities and to other parks. The Grand Tetons, Yellowstone, and Glacier National Parks sequence lends itself nicely to a two-week Grand Tour. It is believed that the establishment of North Cascades National Park will increase the use pressure on Rainier and Olympic National Parks by creating a circular Grand Tour centered on Seattle[36] (Figure 6).

Other professionals suggest that recreational land classification schemes can be used to channel visitors into areas designed to

[36] Catton, "Proposals," pp. 542-543.

withstand heavy use. New York's Adirondack State Park is designed to protect its wilderness core. One million of the park's two million acres are classified as wilderness by federal standards. The small number of primitive trails screens out most users. "Primitive areas" contain occasional nonconforming uses, but the State is phasing these out in an attempt to reclassify all primitive areas as wilderness. "Wild forest" constitutes a little less than half the park. Range cabins, maintenance roads, snowmobile trails, and hiking trails are permitted here. "Recreational areas" constitute one percent of the park's area but absorb most of the visitors. Recreational areas are designed with the social camper in mind and contain boat docks, permanent campgrounds, and other facilities.[37]

Most management suggestions concentrate on facility design and user education. George Craig, a seasoned forestry professional, outlines five major wilderness management problems:

1) *The wilderness timber problem:* Users must be educated out of the live-off-the-land philosophy inherited from an older camping tradition. Lean-tos and bough beds are especially destructive to timber supplies and purists consider them to be extremely unaesthetic. To the extent that purist values regulate behavior in wilderness, the timber problem will diminish.[38]

2) *The recreational stock forage problem:* Craig believes that foot travel is more "primitive" than travel with a string of pack horses, so backpacking should take precedence in crowded wilderness areas. Backpackers are easier on trails, carry their food instead of foraging, and do not mark their route with horse-apples. Mountain meadows are quickly spoiled through trampling and overgrazing. Craig recommends that wilderness managers negotiate agreements with local commercial stock renters and build inconspicuous drift fences to protect fragile areas from grazing.[39]

3) *The wilderness campsite problem:* Campsites should be built away from trails, water bodies, and fragile areas. They should be scattered to disperse users. Each campsite should provide adequate firewood, stock forage, shelter, good water,

---

[37] H.B. Johnson, "The Appalachian Trail and Beyond," *American Institute of Architects Journal*, Vol. 56, October 1971, pp. 23-27.
[38] Craig, "Foresters, Facts, and Philosophy," p. 445.
[39] *Ibid.*, pp. 443-444.

privacy, and safety. Tastefully concealed outhouses, simple split log tables, and rock fireplaces help insulate a campsite against that battered appearance which comes from overuse. Craig observes that for some reason, clean campsites stay clean, and suggests that each be supplied with a rake and a sign with clean-up instructions.[40]

4) *The camping debris problem:* The soil is too shallow in many high country areas to permit trash to be buried. Craig believes that local "wilderness idealists" should be encouraged by managers to publicize the pack-out concept. An individual sense of responsibility is the only solution to the debris problem.[41]

5) *The trails problem:* Most wilderness trails follow old Indian and stockman routes. Grades are often so steep that runoff and erosion problems occur on trails with heavy stock traffic. Granite country requires modern tools for trail building. Neither laborers nor budgets will tolerate the slow hand-construction methods required to avoid conflict with the purist's belief that machines should be excluded from wilderness. Footbridges are often required across boggy meadows to prevent trampling damage, but they, too, intrude on the wilderness.[42] Hendee adds that trails of varied length, type, and quality are needed to a wider variety of places. Most trails should be low to medium in quality: improvements such as dust-reducing wood chip surfaces are not appropriate in wilderness. Trails should be designed for appropriate clientele. Long, steep, primitive trails would appeal to purists, whereas casual day users would tend to pick short, gentle, graded trails. Horses should be kept off hiking trails whenever possible.[43]

The community of purists is trapped by the realities of politics. Successful lobbying requires evidence of support by the voting public. The cultivation of public support requires the popularization of the wilderness ethic. As more people enter the wilderness, it becomes crowded and the wilderness is defaced. It is ironic to note that the sheer size of the community of purists is now one of the chief threats to wilderness preservation. As Leopold pointed out,

---

[40] *Ibid.*
[41] *Ibid.*
[42] *Ibid.*, p. 443.
[43] Hendee *et al., Wilderness Users,* p. 51.

> . . .all conservation of wilderness is self-defeating, for to cherish we must see and fondle, and when enough have seen and fondled, there is no wilderness left to cherish.[44]

The only alternative to loving wilderness to death is management, but "wilderness management" appears to be a contradiction of terms. Dasmann wondered if the final act of wilderness destruction did not lie in designating formal Wilderness Areas for preservation, in defining the boundaries, writing the rules, and publicizing the achievement; what was once remote and unknown was made available to all.[45] On the other hand, in a developed country where all land is used for some purpose, the decision to leave an area untouched must be a management decision. Once wilderness boundaries are drawn, managers become ever more deeply involved in protecting wilderness from its admirers. Two possible management strategies exist. The first is to construct facilities in wilderness which help the land to withstand heavy recreational use. Each facility makes the wilderness easier to penetrate, permitting a larger number of users to enter, and later requiring the construction of more facilities. Managers are required by law to draw the line at roads for motorized vehicles, but a dense network of foot and horse trails with associated facilities would tend to change Wilderness Areas into National Parks. Traditionally, purists have attempted to escape from this dilemma by lobbying for both more National Parks and more Wilderness Areas in order to accommodate the growing recreational demand, and thus to avoid unacceptable management practices in wilderness. Unfortunately, the supply of recreational land is finite (Figure 7).

The second possible management strategy is to manage people rather than land. This strategy may be particularly suited to Wilderness Areas adjacent to major population centers of the Rocky Mountains and Pacific Coast. Mandatory use permits could be used to ration access to wilderness, by spreading a reduced number of users throughout the area to avoid crowding and unacceptable pressure on resources. Social scientists employed by the Forest Service, such as Robert Lucas, believe that public objections to rationed wilderness access would be met

[44] Leopold, *Sand County Sketches*, p. 101.
[45] Dasmann, *Different Kind of Country*, pp. 20-26.

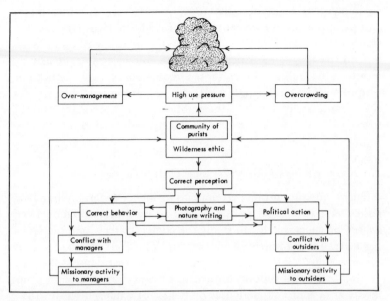

Figure 7   Dynamics of Growth of the Community of Purists

through public education on the impending necessity of the practice.[46]

PURIST PRESSURE GROUPS AND POLITICAL ACTION

As use pressure on the public lands has increased, both policy and administrative options in land management have tended to take on a political aura. As each public lands user group sees its needs rise, it perceives the needs of every other interested group as a threat to the maintenance or expansion of its own share. Accordingly, each major public lands user group has formed an association to make its wishes known to policy-makers and administrators. The political influence of each interested group varies with time, place, and circumstance, whereas the basic incompatibility of their respective land use needs remains constant. Evidently, the political strength of the timber harvest, grazing, mineral development, and recreation-conservation-general resource interest groups is nearly balanced today. Each group is usually able to block legislation or administrative action it finds highly objectionable, but at the same time groups are seldom able

[46] John C. Hendee and Robert C. Lucas, "Mandatory Wilderness Permits: A Necessary Management Tool," *Journal of Forestry*, Vol. 71, April 1973, pp. 206-209.

to implement legislation that one or more of the other major groups opposes. Where events have proved otherwise, the association's success has hinged not only on the intensity of its interest, but on the degree to which it has been able to arouse the usually uninterested public. Under these circumstances, issues tend to be simplified for public judgment and are presented in a manner that dramatically involves the public's value system. The public response is often decisive in a closely balanced political contest.[47]

The Sierra Club and Purist Pressure Group Tactics

Purist pressure groups attempt to influence federal public land policy and to extend public authority over private land. Their degree of success helps to shape the goals, strategy, and tactics of the overall environmental movement. The Sierra Club is widely acknowledged as the most militant and successful purist pressure group.[48] It is the oldest politically aggressive purist organization, involved in lobbying activities on behalf of wilderness from 1892 to the present. The Club has long relied on verbal and visual imagery to present its message to the public. Its literary roots date back to its founder, John Muir, who was one of the best-known American nature writers of the late nineteenth century. The Sierra Club's success, age, and ability to generate images to focus and intensify outward action indicate that the Club has learned to function as a political "elite."

Political scientists recognize a basic difference between "elite" and "mass" forms of political activity. These terms refer not to relative worthiness or status, but to differences in methods, organization, and style. Political elites are highly organized and contain relatively few members. They obtain and use precise information about events which affect their interests and exercise political influence over specifically identified, tangible resources. Elites enjoy a favorable strategic position with respect to both allied and opposing groups, and use rational, cognitive procedures

---

[47] Clawson and Held, *The Federal Lands*, p. 141.
[48] See, for example, articles in the *Atlantic Monthly* (Vol. 228, December 1971, pp. 95-99); *Harper's Magazine* (Vol. 244, March 1972, p. 3); *Business Week* (November 18, 1972, p. 66; May 23, 1970, pp. 64-65; February 21, 1970, p. 39); *New Republic* (Vol. 155, December 3, 1966, p. 7); *Newsweek* (Vol. 68, October 3, 1966, p. 108; Vol. 70, December 25, 1967, p. 50); *Sports Illustrated* (Vol. 30, pp. 36-38+); *Christian Century* (Vol. 89, January 26, 1972, p. 104); and *Holiday* (Vol. 44, December 1968, pp. 58-59+).

to obtain their goals.[49] Elites pursue "practical" politics; that is, they seek specific and tangible benefits which are best obtained by persuading governments to act on their behalf. The link between political acts and consequences is direct, with elite actors constantly checking their actions and assumptions to correct errors and to achieve greater effectiveness.[50] Elites have "staying power:" they are always present and active in the political arena.

In contrast, political masses represent large numbers of people poorly organized for purposeful action. Their "information" consists of stereotyped images which provide an emotional orientation toward events but little specific or exact data about them. Political masses are united by a shared interest in the improvement of their status through protest activity. Their strategic position with respect to political influence is poor, and they are relatively ineffective in securing tangible resources through political activity.[51] For political masses, politics is largely a spectator sport characterized by a flow of dramatic but unconnected images which involve the emotions but have little direct or concrete effect on personal life.[52] Elected officials and other successful political professionals tend to behave as if they believe that most voters are not deeply interested in politics, and that political quiescence and stereotyped reactions rather than a persistent, organized pursuit of interests may be expected from most constituents.[53]

Political elites must solve two related problems: to maintain and increase effectiveness in day-to-day practical politics, and to generate and disseminate political symbols effective in mobilizing mass support in times of crisis. Day-to-day political effectiveness depends in part on the elite's ability to demonstrate to allied and opposing elites that it enjoys mass support. Elites are most successful in mobilizing mass public opinion when elite and mass share common images.[54] Mass public opinion shows little apparent consistency with respect to specific issues and policies,

---

[49] Edelman, *Symbolic Uses of Politics*, p. 36.
[50] *Ibid.*, p. 5.
[51] *Ibid.*, p. 36.
[52] *Ibid.*, p. 5.
[53] *Ibid.*, p. 27.
[54] Edelman, *Politics as Symbolic Action*, p. 10.

but mass attachment to powerful political symbols runs deep.[55] Elite mobilizations of mass opinion may be both skillfully performed and free from cynical exploitation: the elite perceives its action as a call for help on an issue which affects the vital interests of both the elite and the broad public.

The Sierra Club seems to enjoy considerable success in solving both problems. Its practical political effectiveness is widely recognized: the popular press uses such terms as "aggressive,"[56] "militantly conservationist,"[57] "abrasive," and "powerful."[58] *Business Week* called the Sierra Club ". . .the nation's largest and most influential conservation group."[59] The Club's membership, budget, and staff have grown at a dramatic rate since World War II. In 1947, the Club was a fairly parochial California-based hiking and conservation organization with 4,000 members and an annual budget of $100,000. Membership grew throughout the 1960's, with 14,500 members at the beginning of the decade, 47,000 by 1967,[60] and 100,000 in 1970.[61] By the late 1960's, the Club's annual budget reached $2 million.[62] The Sierra Club's evolution from a regional to a national organization is illustrated by the enlistment of new members from regions beyond the Pacific Coast: in 1960, only 750 members lived east of the Mississippi; by 1970, 25,000 members could be found in the Midwest, East Coast, and South.[63] In 1971, the Club employed 102 professional staff members nationwide and had an annual budget of $3.5 million.[64]

The Sierra Club's growing membership, budget, and staff reflect its expanding political horizons. Prior to 1952, the Club lobbied on behalf of new National Parks when necessary, but functioned primarily as a fraternal organization devoted to mountaineering, landscape appreciation, and nature study. In

[55] Philip E. Converse, "The Nature of Belief Systems in Mass Publics," in *Ideology and Discontent,* David Apter (ed.). New York: Free Press, 1964, pp. 206-261.
[56] *Newsweek,* "Fighting Sierrans," Vol. 70, December 25, 1967, p. 50.
[57] *Newsweek,* "Fall from Grace," Vol. 69, January 9, 1967, pp. 24-25.
[58] R.A. Jones, "Fratricide in the Sierra Club," *Nation,* Vol. 208, May 5, 1969, pp. 567-570.
[59] *Business Week,* "Sierra Club Mounts a New Crusade," May 23, 1970, pp. 64-65.
[60] S. Thurber, "Conservation Comes of Age; California Movement," *Nation,* Vol. 204, February 27, 1967, p. 273.
[61] *Business Week,* "Sierra Club's New Crusade," p. 64-65.
[62] Thurber, "Conservation Comes of Age," p. 273.
[63] *Business Week,* "Sierra Club's New Crusade," pp. 64-65.
[64] *New York Times,* "Financial Troubles in Sierra Club," February 20, 1972, p. 3.

1952, the Sierra Club's Board of Directors made the decision to expand its political program through public opposition to a dam proposed for construction in Dinosaur National Monument. The Board considered the dam at Dinosaur a dangerous precedent which threatened to undermine the entire National Park system. David Brower was hired as Executive Director to coordinate the lobbying and media campaigns. Under Brower's leadership in the 1950's and 1960's, the Sierra Club lobbied successfully for the establishment of Redwoods, North Cascades, Canyonlands, and Great Smokies National Parks, and for National Seashores at Cape Cod and Point Reyes. It successfully opposed dams of other development projects that threatened to change the character of existing legally reserved parklands in Dinosaur National Monument, Grand Canyon National Park, the Red River Gorge of Kentucky, Maine's Allagash Wilderness Area, Florida's Everglades National Park, and Storm King Mountain in New York State. The Club's support was instrumental in bringing about such federal legislation as the Wild Rivers Act and the Wilderness Act. In addition, the Club lobbied against development projects which threatened to change natural areas unprotected by National Park status. It opposed dams on the Potomac, Delaware, and Susquehanna Rivers, and on the St. John River in Maine. It opposed a Pacific Gas and Electric Company generating facility proposed for the Pacific Dunes area of California, a resort development in California's Mineral King Valley, and extensive logging in Alaska's Tongass National Forest.[65] By 1970, the Sierra Club was pressing twelve major legal actions and contemplating bringing suit on 100 more issues. Clearly, the Club was ". . .headed far beyond the old definition of conservation."[66]

The struggle to prevent dams from being built in the vicinity of the Grand Canyon may be one of the Club's best known efforts. Brower bought full page advertisements in the *Washington Post* and in the *New York Times* on June 9, 1966 to protest the construction proposals of the federally funded Arizona Water Project. The Internal Revenue Service removed the Sierra Club's tax-exempt status within twenty-four hours of the advertisments' appearance, costing the Club an estimated $125,000 per year in

[65] H. Peterson, "Brower Power Awaits the Verdict," *Sports Illustrated,* Vol. 30, April 14, 1969, pp. 36-38.
[66] *Business Week,* "Sierra Club's New Crusade," p. 64-65.

withheld contributions. This administrative action was taken in advance of any public hearing or investigation and could hardly be called even-handed: the Central Arizona Project Association spent $74,000 in 1965 to advocate the dams the Sierra Club opposed, yet retained its tax-exempt status. Wide media coverage of the Sierra Club's difficulties with the Internal Revenue Service caused Club membership to increase by 25 percent.[67]

Techniques for mobilizing public opinion used by the Sierrra Club reflect John Muir's influence to a very high degree. Muir's prime coincided with the first aggressive phase of the American conservation movement, around 1900. Like many other popular movements, the conservation effort was marked by internal strife. The utilitarian conservationists led by Gifford Pinchot were opposed by the romantic preservationists, led by John Muir. Their differences were crystallized in the U. S. Forest Service and the National Park Service, respectively.[68] Muir realized early that the best way to build support for the National Parks idea was to expose people to the beauty of areas in need of preservation and to define the visitor's experience for him by means of a powerful verbal image. Muir's guided trips through Yosemite became almost as famous as his moving landscape descriptions published by the national press. Later, Muir's wilderness excursions were formalized under his leadership into Sierra Club outings and trips, which are still conducted annually by the Club.[69] Muir's articles appeared in San Francisco newspapers and in national magazines, praising the beauty of Yosemite, excoriating the special interests which threatened to change it, and building support for the National Park idea.

David Brower is widely credited as the moving spirit behind the Sierra Club's new militancy.[70] Responsible only to the Club's Board of Directors, Brower succeeded both in increasing the Club's day-to-day political effectiveness and in disseminating the imagery derived from purist inward action to a broader section of the mass public. The use of imagery to intensify the

---

[67] *Newsweek,* "Fall From Grace," pp. 24-25; and *New Republic,* "Conservationists and the IRS," Vol. 155, December 3, 1966, p. 7.
[68] Roderick Nash, *Wilderness and the American Mind.* New Haven: Yale University Press, 1967, pp. 134-138 *et passim.*
[69] *Ibid.,* p. 129.
[70] See Thurber, "Conservation Comes of Age," p. 273; Peterson, "Brower Power," pp. 36-38; McPhee, *Encounters with the Archdruid,* p. 83; and R. Wernick, "Spoiling for a Good Fight," *Holiday,* Vol. 44, December 1968, pp. 58-59+.

allegiance of existing purists and to mobilize mass public opinion is central to an understanding fo the Club's political methods. The Sierra Club's publishing program, from stationery, wall calendars, and posters to the Exhibit Format Series, attempts to disseminate an image of a "model" wilderness which can be used to judge environmental quality in other landscapes. The Sierra Club and other purist pressure groups have forged a conceptual link between general environmental quality and public access to wilderness in legally reserved parklands. For this reason, environmental activists often use terms such as open space, controlled growth, and environmental protection interchangeably, although the terms in fact refer to quite different goals and tactics. Economic development causes landscape changes incompatible with purist verbal and visual imagery, since developed lands no longer present a Wholly Other contrast to ordinary human existence. A public which accepts purist imagery can be mobilized by purist leaders to combat landscape changes incompatible with the image.

Mobilizing mass public opinion around an image for political purposes requires great skill in the use of mass media. Practical political events are often complex and ambiguous: it is difficult for a public isolated from day-to-day political events to recognize "winners" and "losers" or even to define the issues clearly. Elite leaders attempt to mobilize mass public opinion by presenting an event or issue in terms of a cherished image; therefore, the event or issue must be simplified for public consumption. Dramatic outline virtually requires emptiness of detail.[71] Such simplification is not necessarily cynical. Political events are partially creations of the verbal and visual images used to describe them, and a reporter committed to a certain ideology and its imagery will interpret events for the mass public in the context of his personal beliefs. Skillful use of mass media can forge an association between event and image so strong that they become one in the public mind. Leaders in effect "choose their ground" in political confrontations when they choose critical image/events for presentation to the mass public.

Brower was highly skillful in his ability to link dramatic events with purist imagery to mobilize mass public opinion. Brower's

---

[71] Edelman, *Symbolic Uses of Politics,* pp. 8-9.

critics charged that he was sometimes tempted to "bend the truth" in the name of publicity.

> While Brower was executive director of the Sierra Club, the organization became famous for bold, full-page newspaper ads designed to arouse the populace and written in a style that might be called Early Paul Revere. One such ad called attention to the Kennecott Copper Corporation's ambitions in the Glacier Peak Wilderness under the headline "An Open Pit, Big Enough to be Seen From the Moon." The fact that this was not true did not slow up Brower or the Sierra Club.[72]

An advertisement of this kind may cause criticism from observers inside and outside the community of purists not because it is so unusual in political life, but because such hard-hitting publicity did not become a feature of purist strategy until the late 1960's. Its tone and style are at odds with the traditional high-minded tactics of citizen's reform groups.

Brower represented the radical wing of the Sierra Club. The moderate wing seems to have been represented by the Club's Board of Directors, which voted Brower out of office in 1970. The publication programs and media campaigns required to disseminate purist imagery to the mass public were expensive ventures, and a majority of the Board became convinced that Brower was a poor financial administrator who threatened to bankrupt the Club.[73] In addition, an ideological gap had developed between Brower's "radical" staff and the "moderate" volunteer amateurs of the Board.[74] The Board's basic objection was that Brower's intensity of commitment led him away from the traditional gentlemanly tone and conduct of citizen's groups toward a reliance on propaganda and hard-hitting tactics. Apparently, the Board believed that this approach was detrimental to the Club's long-range interests.[75] Despite the Board's apparent desire to reduce the Sierra Club's activist programs in scope, Brower's innovations were continued by his successor, Michael McCloskey.

"Park Expansion:" The Classic Form of Purist Political Action

"Park expansion" is the classic form of purist political action.

---

[72] McPhee, *Encounters with the Archdruid*, p. 37.
[73] *New York Times*, "Financial Troubles," p. 3.
[74] Jones, "Fratricide," pp. 567-570.
[75] McPhee, *Encounters with the Archdruid*, pp. 200-205.

Its primary purpose is to lobby for the legal reservation of presently undeveloped lands by including them in one of the federal preservation systems. The secondary purpose of park expansion is to guard the character of place in existing parks. Although lands included in the federal preservation systems are in principle permanently closed to most forms of economic development, development threats do arise on occasion. The most dangerous threats, from the purist point of view, are those which involve a clash between two versions of the public good in the treatment of a potential park site.

Many of the characteristics of park expansion as a form of purist political action emerged in the early twentieth century during the famous Hetch Hetchy controversy. The City of San Francisco sought permission from the federal government to build a dam at the mouth of Hetch Hetchy Valley in the northern section of Yosemite National Park, in order to supply water and hydroelectric power to the city's municipal system. John Muir organized and led national opposition to the plan. To him, the threat to the park's supposed inviolability was an image/event which summarized many related issues in the treatment of the American landscape. Muir identified preservation of the valley with a vote of confidence in spiritual and aesthetic values and dam construction with materialism and irreverence toward God's Creation.[76] To Muir, industrial development and careless agriculture were signs of spiritual death. He attacked the motives of the development interests in a stream of articles in the national press. Controversy continued for five years, until on December 6, 1913 the Senate voted narrowly to permit construction of the dam.[77]

Toward the end of the controversy, Senator James A. Reed of Missouri observed that the intensity of resistance to the dam increased with the distance from its site, to peak in the transcendental heartland of New England.[78] Reed felt that this geographic imbalance in public opinion indicated that the Hetch Hetchy controversy was a spurious issue, since under a federal system of government local issues should be decided at the local level. Political philosophy aside, Reed's observation recognizes

[76] Roderick Nash (ed.), *The Call of the Wild: 1900-1916.* New York: George Braziller, 1970, pp. 12-15.
[77] *Ibid.*
[78] *Ibid.*

scale differences common to many developer-preservationist clashes. Local ecomonic interests often perceive issues at the "large scale," since they possess detailed but narrowly focused knowledge of the park's potential contribution to local prosperity. A park site's contribution to a national economy is small, and in the absence of direct financial interest, the geographically dispersed membership of the community of purists perceives the issues at the small scale, with few details about a local economy but with broad implications for the human condition.

Political battles over park expansion tend to follow a basic pattern. First, purist leaders learn that development interests have begun to advocate a project which would change an existing park or develop potential parklands for the first time. Whether developers plan a ski resort, a copper mine, or a timber harvest, purist leaders resolve to obstruct and prevent the proposed project. News of the impending danger spreads through the community of purists via meeting and newsletter, and a coalition of groups and individuals organizes for action. Purist leaders may initiate the conflict with a lawsuit or with an appeal to the appropriate legislative or administrative body. Simultaneously, purist leaders attempt to use mass media to present the issue as an image/event important to the overall preservationist cause. The developers respond with public statements on the utility of the project, citing its potential contribution to local employment opportunities and tax bases, and stressing the industry's role in maintaining national prosperity. Environmental changes which the developers presume to be small and unimportant are contrasted with the potential benefits of economic growth. Purist leaders not only extol the unique qualities of the potential park site but also raise the principle that an assault on the integrity of any wilderness is a threat to the entire preservation system. As litigation works its way through the courts, legislative body, or administrative hierarchy, political strategies and legal/administrative procedural moves become increasingly difficult to distinguish. When a decision is finally reached—a process which may take decades, as in the case of the Hells Canyon National Recreation Area[79]—the victorious interest emerges with increased political power and expertise.

[79] John E. Simonds, "Symms Loses Fight to Delay Hell's Canyon Action," *Idaho Statesman*, September 11, 1975, p. 11.

The achievement of a declared political objective not only fails to put to rest the political interest in question, but also leads to the advancement of more ambitious claims of the same general character as the satisfied claim.[80] President Johnson signed the Wilderness Act into law in 1964; in the following five years, 167 areas were added to the Wilderness Preservation System. The late 1960's also witnessed a rapid evolution in purist political goals and tactics. Park expansion remained an important goal, but traditional purist interests tended to be overshadowed by a new program, "development control."

"Development Control:" A Recent Innovation in Purist Political Action

"Development control" is a form of purist political action which attempts to apply something approaching wilderness standards to settled landscapes. No attempt is made to include the controversial area in a new park. Development control goals and tactics may be applied to any area unprotected by park status, but most development control controversies occur over resource development issues in the middle landscape. Leo Marx invented the term "middle landscape" to signify the land use and settlement patterns intermediate between the man-made city and the unchanged wilderness.[81] Although the dominant image of the middle landscape is agricultural, here Marx's definition will be loosened to include all land uses associated with the primary economic sector. Development control is both a political program and an intellectual position. Its rationale depends on the fusion of the wilderness ethic and the land ethic described earlier. The wilderness ethic is primarily a code based on the avoidance of land use, whereas the land ethic preaches wise land use. Leopold defined "wise" as gentle, ecologically sound practices derived from scientific study of the natural order and from emotional attachment to the land. An essential part of this wisdom was the ability to recognize those areas which were best left untouched; hence Leopold's association with the community of purists. Essentially, however, the land ethic is a philosophy for the middle landscape.

---

[80] Edelman, *Symbolic Uses of Politics*, p. 153.
[81] Leo Marx, *The Machine in the Garden: Technology and the Pastoral Ideal in America.* New York: Oxford University Press, 1964, *passim.*

Development control rests philosophically on a special interpretation of Leopold's thought: intensive land use and gentle, ecologically sound land use are mutually exclusive categories. The more thorough the land use, the more land declines from the axiomatic perfection of wilderness. The wilderness ethic postulates wilderness as the ideal condition for Earth, the way it was fresh from the Creator's hands. If one accepts this interpretation of Leopold's position, it follows that wise land use is reduced land use. Of course, not all land can be wilderness, but development control attempts to use political influence to place more land in uses which approach the axiomatic ideal.

Development control is closely related to park expansion when the goal is preservation of wilderness as wilderness. Postwar prosperity caused a dramatic increase in use pressure on the middle landscape. Although contradictory trends existed, such as rural depopulation and farmland retirement to the Soil Bank, in general it was a period of increasingly thorough land use. Use pressure forced the middle landscape to spread into areas that had been *de facto* wilderness, in the sense that they had not been needed for any economic purpose. The postwar militance of the community of purists can be understood partially as an attempt to erect legal levees around remaining wilderness areas to prevent them from being flooded by the middle landscape.

The more important aspect of development control, however, is the struggle to define the "correct" level of intensity in middle landscape land use. If intensive land use is believed to be necessarily equivalent to environmental degradation, environmental protection must require either an end to the offending land use or a reform of the land use method. Accumulating scientific evidence of the dangers of environmental degradation has provided robust support for general purist goals, but the evidence does not necessarily support the position that intensive land use is inherently harmful.

Development control builds on the traditions of park expansion, predisposing the community of purists more to prevention than to reform. Since the late 1960's, purist leaders have learned to take advantage of the multiplicity of new, untried environmental protection legislation. Lawsuits can be used to force compliance with environmental legislation and thus to establish precedents for additional decisions favorable to the purist cause.

This tactic resembles the methods of the civil rights movement, which learned to roll up the next legislative hill under the momentum of favorable court decisions. Although litigation is a traditional tool used by pressure groups across the entire political spectrum, the volume of purist litigation since the late 1960's justifies the comment in *Business Week* that lawsuits to protect the public's right to a clean environment must be considered a "new weapon."[8 2]

The Admiralty Island case and the Mineral King case provide examples of purist litigation to achieve development control. The Sierra Club brought its third action against the U. S. Forest Service in less than a year, when in 1970 the Club announced that it would sue to prevent U. S. Plywood-Champion International Corporation from erecting a $75 million timber processing facility at Berner's Bay, 42 miles from Juneau. The plant was needed to process timber from the Admiralty Island timber sale.

Admiralty Island is both prime wildlife habitat for bald eagles, blacktail deer, and brown bears, and prime hemlock and Sitka spruce forest. In early 1968, Champion International Corporation purchased rights from the Forest Service to clear-cut nearly the entire 1,703 square miles of Admiralty Island and nearby lands, all within Tongass National Forest. This contract represented the largest single timber sale in the history of the Forest Service, valued in 1974 at $140 million.

The Sierra Club challenged the sale in court, arguing that the contract violated federal law requiring multiple use of National Forests, recreation and wildlife habitat preservation as well as provision of timber. The U. S. District Court which heard the case ruled in favor of Champion, but when the Sierra Club came across a study by two forest ecologists from the University of California, it decided to resubmit its complaint.

The study, originally commissioned by Champion International, found that clear-cutting would destroy virtually all the island's wildlife habitat and suggested that a more restrained cutting plan be substituted. The report was so damaging that the Sierra Club persuaded the circuit court to order a new trial in Juneau. Eventually, the Club hoped to spark a congressional fight with timber interests over clear-cutting.[8 3]

[8 2] *Business Week*, "Sierra Club's New Crusade, pp. 64-65.
[8 3] Herbert G. Lawson, "Critics Step Up Battle With Timber Industry Over Logging Methods," *Wall Street Journal,* January 24, 1974, p. 1.

The Sierra Club's arguments were based on economic, environmental, and chauvinistic issues.[84] According to Sierra Club attorneys, the market appraisal on which the timber sale was based was outdated; therefore, the Forest Service had violated its own regulations by selling timber below its full market value. The Club also argued that clear-cutting could not be considered a form of multiple use, nor could the timber sale be presumed to contribute to national wood products needs, since the bulk of the harvest would be sold to Japan.[85] As yet, the case is unresolved.

Mineral King Valley is located about 170 miles north of Los Angeles, adjacent to Sequoia National Park. The Forest Service believed the valley to be particularly suited for development as a ski resort, and encouraged Walt Disney Productions to draft a project proposal. Disney Productions envisioned a pseudo-Austrian "Alpine Village" capable of processing several thousand visitors per day, year round. The project required an access road through Sequoia National Park, the only feasible route.[86]

On June 5, 1969, the Sierra Club intervened with a suit seeking preliminary and permanent injunctions against the project. The first part of the suit named the Forest Service and the Secretary of Agriculture as defendents. The Club's attorneys argued that Congress had set eighty acres as the maximum size for resorts developed under lease on National Forest land, but that the Forest Service had attempted to circumvent this requirement by granting Disney year-to-year leases on 300 acres more. This 300 acres was to be altered permanently by construction of the "village" and its associated facilities. Furthermore, the 300 acres belonged to the Sequoia National Game Refuge and the Club estimated that 13,000 more acres of game refuge land would be significantly affected by the construction of ski runs, lifts, and gondolas. The suit charged that the lease arrangement constituted a clear violation of federal law and the Forest Service's own regulations.[87]

[84] *Business Week,* "U.S. Plywood's Forest of Trouble; Sale of Timber from Tongass National Forest," February 21, 1970, p. 39.
[85] *Ibid.*
[86] *Newsweek,* "Mom vs. Apple Pie; Opposes Disney's Proposed Alpine Village," Vol. 73, February 10, 1969, p. 25.
[87] P. Browning, "Mickey Mouse in the Mountains," *Harper's Magazine,* Vol. 244, No. 3, March 1972, p. 3.

A second set of charges named the National Park Service and the Secretary of the Interior as defendents. The Disney project required highway access, yet the only possible route would cut across a portion of Sequoia National Park. Federal legislation requires that all road construction in National Parks must serve park purposes; the Club argued that an access road to the Disney project would violate this requirement.[88]

The Sierra Club obtained a preliminary injunction against the project on July 23, 1969 from District Court Judge William T. Sweigert. Judge Sweigert ruled that serious legal issues were at stake and that the Club had legal standing to bring a class action suit. The Forest Service appealed Sweigert's decision and won, when the appeals court ruled that the Sierra Club did not have legal standing to sue, because the Club could not demonstrate that the Disney project would harm any of its members in any fashion. The Club appealed to the United States Supreme Court, which upheld the appeals court decision in a 4-3 decision. The Supreme Court based its decision on the standing issue, and ruled that the Sierra Club did not have the right to sue on behalf of the general public. By basing its decision on a narrow procedural issue, the Court virtually invited the Sierra Club to amend its complaint and try again.[89]

The Sierra Club had hoped to enlarge its legal standing with a precedent-setting victory in the Mineral King case and thus open up vast new realms of litigation possibilities. The Mineral King case was partly a symbolic issue. The Forest Service hoped to use the Disney proposals as a model for future recreational development projects. To the Sierra Club, Mineral King was a test issue on the limits of administrative authority. The Forest Service, Disney Productions, and the Sierra Club all claimed to act in the best interests of conservation. The Forest Service defined "conservation" as the use of public lands to produce revenue, Disney Productions as investment opportunities, and the Sierra Club as the act of leaving well enough alone.

Both park expansion and development control are forms of "defensive warfare,"[90] since both strategies attempt to prevent land use changes in wilderness areas. The goal of park expansion

---

[88] *Ibid.*
[89] *Ibid.*
[90] Thurber, "Conservation Comes of Age," p. 275.

is to declare an area "off limits" by including it in one of the federal preservation systems. Obviously, all land is not and cannot be wilderness, so the Sierra Club favors a type of zoning concept: ninety percent of the land for economic purposes, ten percent for wilderness.[91] Growing problems of environmental degradation and the Sierra Club's expanding political influence have encouraged purists to turn their attention from exclusive pursuit of wilderness preservation to the other ninety percent, the settled landscape. "Development control" builds on the traditions of park expansion, to create an intellectual position and political program with major implications for the overall environmental movement.

THE WILDERNESS ETHIC AND THE ENVIRONMENTAL MOVEMENT

The wilderness ethic is the most completely articulated version of the "correct" relationship between man and nature with widespread current public appeal. For this reason, imagery and values derived from the wilderness ethic tend to spill over into environmental questions where they may not be useful or appropriate. This spillover effect is caused partly by the political effectiveness of purist pressure groups, and partly by the intellectual and emotional effectiveness of purist imagery. It has been said that the power of Marxist ideology may be measured by the necessity for conservatives to use Marxist terminology to discuss the ideas they oppose. Marxist ideology, as a powerful mode of perception, tends to supplant other modes or reduce them to a defensive position. In a somewhat similar fashion, the wilderness ethic has influenced the environmental movement. The purist mode of perception has been powerful enough to pervade public discussion of overall environmental issues such as pollution, overpopulation, and resource depletion. Most important, the ability of the wilderness ethic to flow into other aspects of the environmental movement is aided by the erosion of positive spiritual and aesthetic values associated with the countryside and the city.

Many Americans seem to view the city largely in terms of its problems. A mild urban nausea seems to be accepted by many as inevitable, a venerable point of view in American culture. The

[91] David Brower, "Introduction," in Brower (ed.), *Wilderness: America's Living Heritage*, p. vii.

wilderness ethic may inadvertently contribute to the low value placed on the city. In the eighteenth and nineteenth centuries, the American rejection of the city led to an embrace of the family farm as an idealized alternative environment. Today, the myth of the family farm seems to be losing potency as farm life becomes an ever more remote and romanticized memory for most Americans. A contemporary urbanite's discontent with his environment cannot be interrrupted by farm experience unless he is wealthy enough to afford a hobby farm or a dude ranch vacation. In contrast, Wilderness Areas and National Parks are accessible to anyone with a two-week vacation. An environmental myth cannot flourish without an opportunity for personal experience in the alternative environment, even if the personal experience is highly conventionalized. Ansel Adams' concept of "presentation" is useful here: national and state park systems present wild nature almost exclusively. Since personal contact with the world outside the city is available to many only through brief vacations on dude ranches or in some sort of legally reserved area on the model of a National Park, it follows that many urbanites are trained to perceive wild scenery as the most positive aspect of the landscape.

Raymond Williams suggests that British radicals opposed to industrial capitalism have traditionally contrasted the squalid, ruthless city with an idealized vision of "moral" and "natural" rural life. Such political radicals tend to be attached to country ways, feelings, and lore, and hostile to industrialism and commercialism.[92] They honor the "timeless rural rhythm"[93] and oppose the alienation from nature and society believed to be caused by life in large urban centers. (However, the feudal society they idealize had in reality exploitative attributes and the countryside, far from being "timeless," was always changing.[94]) Williams believes that many members of the British urban middle classes hold this idealized view, but in a less intense form and without any radical political context. A picturesque convention about the British countryside exists: subjects of interest include natural history, practical land management, quaint old country

[92] Raymond Williams, *The Country and the City*. New York: Oxford University Press, 1973, pp. 36-37.
[93] *Ibid.*, pp. 9-12.
[94] *Ibid.*

sayings, outdoor anecdotes, community histories, remodeled country cottages, fine drawings, photographs, and landscape descriptions.[9 5]

A parallel rural nostalgia exists in the United States, although it honors the pioneer experience rather than feudal society. The pioneer carved a homestead from the wilderness: if public nostalgia focuses on the homestead's wilderness setting, the heroic athleticism of purist personal behavior in wilderness becomes a way of preserving the pioneer spirit in a contemporary context. The Boy Scout movement of the early twentieth century proposed to preserve the American national character by inculcating youth with pioneer values through ritualistic reenactments of pioneer experiences.[9 6] Once the purist behavior and pioneer values are amalgamated, nostalgic nationalism and anti-urban sentiments reinforce both the intellectual and emotional aspects of purist imagery.

The wilderness ethic makes a strict division between productive land and land reserved for spiritual/aesthetic enjoyment: the ninety percent used for economic purposes is an inferior environment by definition; wilderness areas alone preserve environmental excellence. Williams points out that eighteenth century English landscaping was based on a parallel division between land for production and land for consumption. The straight roads and hedges of the newly enclosed lands were contemporaneous with naturalistic landscape gardening. Laborers and tenants worked the land organized for production; owners enjoyed leisured repose and fine views on land organized for consumption. The creation of "fine views" required an abstract and generalized countryside, where evidences of production were banished in favor of well designed woods, meadows, and lakes.[9 7] In a similar sense, if wilderness areas are models for general environmental excellence, landscapes associated with production are condemned because of their weak spiritual and aesthetic associations. The wilderness ethic itself is not necessarily opposed to the alternative environments of countryside and city; it becomes opposed only when values derived from the wilderness ethic are used to judge environmental quality in settled landscapes.

[9 5] *Ibid.*, p. 262.
[9 6] Nash, *Call of the Wild, passim.*
[9 7] Williams, *The Country and the City*, pp. 124-125.

The public view of man-nature relationships is necessarily built into any environmental policy goal. The rallying cry of the environmental movement is "quality of life." If quality of life is to become a useful public policy index, it cannot become too impossibly utopian in its definition. Quality of life cannot limit itself to wilderness-like models for the other two landscapes without ignoring the problem of livelihood. Livelihood will always be served by public policy; the problem is that an overly broad application of wilderness criteria can lead environmental activists to the position that economic development and intensive land use are necessarily forms of environmental degradation. This position requires political action in favor of wilderness to be negative and reactive in character, and undercuts the intellectual effort needed to plan forms of economic development and intensive land use which are ecologically and aesthetically harmonious with the landscape. The danger of the wilderness ethic is identical to the danger inherent in any other ideology: it can be applied inflexibly.

A resurgence of interest in the spiritual and aesthetic aspects of the countryside and the city is needed to balance the wilderness ethic. The magnitude of the purist achievement can be appreciated if one contrasts the Sierra Club's formidable membership, budget, staff, publication program, and litigation campaign with the absence of any parallel organization devoted to environmental quality in settled landscapes. A "Manhattan Club" or a "Friends of the Exurban Fringe" seems both impossible and comic, yet perhaps environmental conservation efforts might make more rapid progress if such organizations existed.

Architects, landscape architects, and planners have developed a group perception of urban environmental quality; the influential journal *Landscape* did much to develop a similar viewpoint for rural environments. At present, however, models of environmental quality specific to settled landscapes are confined largely to professional circles. Professional value judgments have not been transformed into powerful imagery by artists and writers, nor have politically effective national organizations attempted to disseminate positive environmental images among the public, much less to mobilize public opinion in favor of urban and rural environmental reform. Environmental activists interested in the conservation of settled landscapes have much to learn from purist tactics. The opportunity to alternate among three contrasting environments contributes to the richness and variety of emotional life. Contrast value is heightened by imagery which summarizes and evokes the spirit of place which can be ascribed to each landscape. In this sense, the wilderness ethic makes a major contribution to American culture.

IV

Summary and Conclusions: Six Themes

RELIGIOUS FEELING IN SECULAR DRESS

T he wilderness ethic is strongly religious in character. Wilderness is treated as sacred space by the community of purists, whether or not purists consciously accept the notion of wilderness as hierophany. Abbey considers himself an atheist, Krutch was an agnostic, at one time Adams denied or apologized for the spiritual quality of his photographs; yet none of these artists can quite escape his own preoccupation with sacred power. If one believes that wilderness is a manifestation of sacred power and a zone which contributes to receptivity to numinous experience, he gains a fixed point, or center, which stands out from the chaotic relativity of ordinary life. To the purist, wilderness is a manifestation of the Absolute, yet it is concrete, visible, and close at hand. He can immerse himself in perfection (if only for a weekend) and emerge purified. This is strong medicine: when the wilderness ethic is seen in its religious context, it is easier to understand the emotional heat generated in purist political struggles.

THE NEED FOR ORDER

The wilderness ethic is an axiomatic system of feeling and belief. Like all axiomatic systems, it is arranged like a pyramid, with a first cause at the apex and a host of implications at the base. In the case of the wilderness ethic, the apex is sacred power and the base is purist recommendations to managers and policy-makers. Because wilderness is believed to be a manifestation of sacred power, any man-made change pulls wilderness down from its peak of perfection. Therefore, the value and beauty of wilderness is precisely that it is the Wholly Other opposite from man. As Kurt Gödel first pointed out, any axiomatic system is also a normative system: goals of some sort are built into its structure.[1] In the wilderness ethic, the community of purists is the means to the ends of protecting wilderness in parks and extending wilderness values to other landscapes.

Both theology and science attempt to study different aspects of the order built into the world, but the manner in which intellectual systems evolve or disappear suggests that the order is as much man-imposed as natural. Nature writers and landscape photographers have not yet succeeded in filling in the entire axiomatic structure of the wilderness ethic. They are engaged in a continuous struggle to establish canons of perception and behavior by resolving the contradictions which remain. Despite internal contradictions, difficulties of application, and the impermanence of intellectual systems, the faith that one has found the true order can be an inspiration to action which might otherwise seem much too difficult.

THE NEED FOR COMMUNITY

The purist is a self-conscious observer of landscapes. He not only looks at wilderness but is conscious that he is doing so as an experience in itself.[2] His act of vision is supported and justified by a set of social models and analogies from science, art, literature, and history. The wilderness ethic is a creation not of nature but of a human community. Organization helps purists to find one another, to develop allegiance to the group, to adopt a group code of behavior in wilderness, and to achieve political effectiveness. The fraternal and political functions community of purists are profoundly intertwined: wilderness sports, nature study, and landscape appreciation are simultaneously enjoyable forms of recreation and an act of allegiance to purist values.

[1] Ernest Nagel and James R. Newman, *Gödel's Proof*. New York: New York University Press, 1964, *passim*.
[2] Raymond Williams, *The Country and the City*. New York: Oxford University Press, 1973, p. 121.

THE NEED FOR AN IMAGE

Intellectual order alone is too austere to stimulate the emotional energy necessary for religious belief. Communal ties reinforce intellectual belief, but purists also need to carry a picture of wilderness in their minds which is consistent with the axiom and corollaries of the wilderness ethic. The image of wilderness has evolved rapidly, and today "ecologically sound," "beautiful," "natural," "perfect," and "wild" are synonyms in purist discourse. Wilderness imagery is derived from pictorial criteria traditional to landscape painting; from an aesthetic orientation toward the natural sciences, particularly ecology; and from the efforts of purist nature writers and landscape photographers who attempt to portray wilderness as it appears to a mind in the midst of transcendent experience. Paul Shepard's "unparklike parks" can now be added to the national preservation system because of the partial public acceptance of purist imagery. If any landscape is beautiful so long as it is wild, lands worthy of preservation no longer need resemble the traditional pastoral image of nature as the gentleman's park. Wilderness imagery both gives aesthetic form to purist inward action and serves as an "education of vision," where acceptance of purist verbal and visual imagery prepares an observer to accept purist intellectual positions and political goals.

The image may be more important than axiomatic order in training the purist's perception of wilderness along correct lines. If proper perception is learned, does it follow that the wilderness experience is an illusion? The wilderness experience is not a primal feeling in the sense of hunger or pain, although the axiomatic structure of the wilderness ethic suggests that this ought to be true. Rather, the surge of emotion the purist feels in wilderness is a cultural experience with a religious core. The religious core could be served as well by any other ritual or symbol, but wilderness is one of the symbols that has chanced to evolve in American culture. The surge of patriotic emotion at a parade is a perfectly genuine secular emotion which is learned rather than inherent. The wilderness experience is genuine in the same sense.

THE NEED FOR ACTION

Political involvement plays a central role in the wilderness ethic for three reasons. First, the axiomatic structure of the wilderness ethic implies political goals. Second, personal experience in wilderness and dramatic political confrontations function as rituals which both strengthen the allegiance of present purists and help to attract new members to the community. Third, political goals tend to spread in scope with advances in organizational effectiveness. Political pressure groups attempt to aim high, to become bigger, better, and more effective, to use each victory as a springboard toward greater political objectives.

Unfortunately, effective political action has led purist pressure groups into two difficult positions. "Park expansion" cannot continue indefinitely because the supply of recreational land is finite. Successful lobbying requires evidence of support by the mass public. Cultivation of public support requires popularization of the wilderness ethic. As more and more users enter the wilderness, it becomes crowded and wilderness values are destroyed. The only alternative to destruction by use pressure is management, which either imposes strict controls on user numbers and behavior or introduces artifacts to protect wilderness from its admirers. Regulations and artifacts are at odds with the Wholly Other quality purists value in wilderness, and tend to remove wilderness from its axiomatic perfection to a lower state like that of a National Park or a National Forest. "Development control" efforts have led purists to a second difficult position. Urban and rural landscapes are creations of the search for livelihood, which necessarily requires sweeping landscape changes. The wilderness ethic is primarily a philosophy based on the avoidance of man-caused environmental changes, so the application of wilderness criteria to questions of environmental quality in settled landscapes tends to force purists into a negative and reactive political stance. The wilderness image simply does not lend itself well to use as a conceptual base for quality judgments on the type, location, intensity, or pattern of environmental locations in settled landscapes.

OTHER LANDSCAPES

Wilderness, garden, and city are distinct environmental ideals which have appeared in many cultures widely scattered in time and space. Tuan has shown that the three environments tend to have ambiguous meanings which shift over time, but nevertheless serve as powerful symbols of life. Each environmental ideal can be defined only in contrast to the other two.[3]

Superficially, the wilderness ethic is concerned with wilderness alone, but in fact it depends on the other two landscapes for intellectual, political, and emotional definition. Leopold's land ethic is a philosophy for the middle landscape, or garden. The land ethic fuses with the wilderness ethic when wise land use includes the ability to recognize which areas are best left untouched; and when gentle, ecologically sound land management methods are regarded as incompatible with industrial development and intensive land use. These special interpretations of the land ethic constitute the basic assumptions of park expansion and development control, respectively, and are used to justify purist pressure group efforts to prevent wilderness areas from being engulfed by the middle landscape.

The city influences wilderness in the person of the purist, for the wilderness ethic is an urban phenomenon reflecting both the educated city dweller's cultivated sensibility and his lack of contact with the means of rural livelihood. For this reason political support for wilderness preservation often increases with distance from the potential park site. This geographical imbalance does not invalidate the wilderness ethic; it merely highlights the differences in perception and means of livelihood which often separate urban and rural residents.

The verbal and visual imagery associated with the wilderness ethic yields a high degree of emotional definition. At present, wilderness imagery helps guide many Americans to intense commitment to preservation of the wilderness environment, but comparable imagery for the countryside or city appears to be weak or non-existent. Much of the political influence of the community of purists stems from the ability of wilderness imagery to flow into the void left by the erosion of spiritual and aesthetic values associated with the countryside and city. Partially by default, partially by political expertise, and partially by strength of conviction, the wilderness ethic and its purist supporters continue to attract adherents and to influence the direction of the environmental movement through the power of a single concept, wilderness as sacred space.

---

[3] Yi-Fu Tuan, *Topophilia: A Study in Environmental Perception, Attitudes, and Values.* Englewood Cliffs, N.J.: Prentice-Hall, Inc., 1974, pp. 129-149.

Bibliography

ABBEY, EDWARD, *Desert Solitaire: A Season in the Wilderness*, New York: Ballantine Books, Inc., 1971.

ADAMS, ANSEL and NANCY NEWHALL, *This is the American Earth*, San Francisco: Sierra Club, 1960.

American Forests, "Kick the Exploiters Out of the Wilderness Temple," Vol. 68, No. 10, October 1962, pp. 15+.

ASCHMANN, H., "People, Recreation, Wildlands, and Wilderness," *Landscape*, Vol. 18, No. 1, Winter 1969, pp. 40-44.

BALLANTINE, GRAEME E., "Planning for Remoteness," *Town Planning Institute Journal*, Vol. 57, February 1971, pp. 60-64.

BLUHM, WILLIAM T., *Ideologies and Attitudes: Modern Political Culture*, Englewood Cliffs, N.J.: Prentice-Hall, Inc., 1974.

BROOKS, PAUL, "Warnings: The Chain Saw Cometh," *Atlantic Monthly*, Vol. 228, No. 6, December 1971, pp. 95-99.

BROWER, DAVID (ed.), *Going Light—With Backpack or Burro*, San Francisco: Sierra Club, 1951.

_____, *The Meaning of Wilderness to Science: Proceedings, Sixth Biennial Wilderness Conference*, San Francisco: Sierra Club, 1959.

_____, *Wilderness: America's Living Heritage: Wilderness Conference Proceedings*, San Francisco: Sierra Club, 1961.

_____, *Wildlands in Our Civilization*, San Francisco: Sierra Club, 1964.

BROWNING, P., "Mickey Mouse in the Mountains," *Harper's Magazine*, Vol. 244, No. 3, March 1972, p. 3.

_____, "Commentary: California's Mineral King Valley," *Harper's Magazine*, Vol. 245, No. 8, August 1972, pp. 102-103.

BULTENA, GORDON L. and MARION J. TAVES, "Changing Wilderness Images and Forest Policy," *Journal of Forestry*, Vol. 59, 1961, pp. 167-171.

BURCH, WILLIAM R. JR., "The Play World of Camping: Research Into the Social Meaning of Outdoor Recreation," *American Journal of Sociology*, Vol. 70, 1965, pp. 604-612.

_____, *The Social Characteristics of Participants in Three Styles of Family Camping*, U.S. Forest Service, Pacific Northwest Forest and Range Experiment Station, Research Paper PNW-48, 1967.

Business Week, "U.S. Plywood's Forest of Trouble; Sale of Timber from Tongass National Forest," February 21, 1970, p. 39.

_____, "Sierra Club Mounts a New Crusade," May 23, 1970, pp. 64-65.

_____, "Truce in the Western Strip Mining War; New Mexico's Coal Surface Mining Act," November 18, 1972, p. 66.

CAHART, ARTHUR H. (ed.), *Planning for America's Wildlands*, Harrisburg, Pa.: Telegraph Press, for the National Audubon Society, National Parks Association, Wilderness Society, and Wildlife Management Institute, 1961.

CATTON, WILLIAM R. JR., "The Proposals as Viewed by a Sociologist, *Journal of Forestry*, Vol. 66, July 1968, pp. 540-546.

CLARK, KENNETH, *Landscape Into Art*, London: John Murray, Ltd., 1949.

CLAWSON, MARION and BURNELL HELD, *The Federal Lands: Their Use and Management*, Baltimore: The Johns Hopkins University Press, for Resources for the Future, Inc., 1957.

CLIFF, E.P., "Reply with Rejoinder," *Atlantic Monthly*, Vol. 229, No. 2, February 1972, pp. 37-38.

CLIFFORD, RICHARD J., *The Cosmic Mountain in Canaan and the Old Testament*, Cambridge, Mass.: Harvard University Press, 1972.

COKE, VAN DEREN, "Taos and Santa Fe," *Art in America*, May 1963, pp. 44-47.

CONVERSE, PHILIP E., "The Nature of Belief Systems in Mass Publics," in *Ideology and Discontent*, David Apter (ed.), New York: Free Press, 1964, pp. 206-261.

CORBETT, PATRICK, *Ideologies*, New York: Harcourt, Brace and World, Inc., 1965.

CRAIG, GEORGE A., "Foresters, Facts, and Philosophy in the Resource Policy Mix," *Journal of Forestry*, Vol. 64, October 1966, pp. 664-667.

DASMANN, RAYMOND F., *A Different Kind of Country*, New York: The Macmillan Company, 1968.

EDELMAN, MURRAY, *The Symbolic Uses of Politics*, Urbana: University of Illinois Press, 1964.

_____, *Politics as Symbolic Action: Mass Arousal and Quiescence*, Chicago: Markham Publishing Company, for the Institute for Research on Poverty, Monograph Series, 1971.

ELIADE, MIRCEA, *Images and Symbols: Studies in Religious Symbolism*, New York: Sheed and Ward, 1961.

_____, *The Sacred and the Profane: The Nature of Religion*, New York: Harper Torchbooks, 1961.

ELLUL, JACQUES, *Propaganda: The Formation of Men's Attitudes*, New York: Alfred A. Knopf, 1965.

Environmental Studies Division, Office of Research and Monitoring, Environmental Protection Agency, *Quality of Life Indicators: A Review of the State of the Art and Guidelines Derived to Assist in Developing Environmental Indicators*, Washington, D. C.: Government Printing Office, 1972.

FIREY, W., "Sentiment and Symbolism as Ecological Variables," in *Studies in Human Ecology*, G. A. Theodorson (ed.), Evanston, Ill.: Harper and Row, 1961, pp. 253-262.

FRISSELL, SIDNEY S. JR. and GEORGE H. STANKEY, "Wilderness Environmental Quality: Search for Social and Ecological Harmony," *Proceedings*, Society of American Foresters Annual Meeting, Hot Springs, Arkansas, 1972, pp. 170-183.

GILBERT, C. GORMAN *et al.*, "Toward a Model of Travel Behavior in the Boundary Waters Canoe Area," *Environment and Behavior*, June 1972, pp. 132-157.

GRAD, FRANK P., GEORGE W. RUTHJENS, and ALBERT J. ROSENTHAL, *Environmental Control: Priorities, Policies, and the Law*, New York: Columbia University Press, 1971.

GREGORY, MICHAEL, "Ansel Adams: The Philosophy of Light," *Aperture*, Vol. 2, No. 2, February 1964, pp; 49-51.

HANO, A., "Protectionists vs. Recreationists; the Battle of Mineral King," *New York Times Magazine,* August 17 1969, pp. 24-25.

HEBERLEIN, T. A., "Land Ethic Realized: Some Changing Environmental Attitudes," *Journal of Social Issues,* Vol. 28, No. 4, pp. 79-87.

HENDEE, JOHN C. *et al., Wilderness Users in the Pacific Northwest: Their Characteristics, Values, and Management Preferences,* U.S. Forest Service, Pacific Northwest Forest and Range Experiment Station, Research Paper PNW-61.

HENDEE, JOHN C. and FREDERICK L. CAMPBELL, "Social Aspects of Outdoor Recreation: The Developed Campground," *Trends in Parks and Recreation,* Vol. 6, October 1969, pp. 13-16.

HENDEE, JOHN C. and ROBERT W. HARRIS, "Foresters' Perception of Wilderness User Attitudes and Preferences," *Journal of Forestry,* Vol. 68, December 1970, pp. 759-762.

HENDEE, JOHN C. and ROBERT C. LUCAS, "Mandatory Wilderness Permits: A Necessary Management Tool," *Journal of Forestry,* Vol. 71, April 1973, pp. 206-209.

HUSSEY, CHRISTOPHER, *The Picturesque: Studies in a Point of View,* London: Frank Cass and Company, Ltd., 1967.

ISAAC, ERICH, "God's Acre," in *The Subversive Science: Essays Toward an Ecology of Man,* PAUL SHEPARD and DANIEL McKINLEY (eds.), Boston: Houghton Mifflin Company, 1969, pp. 149-158.

JACKSON, JOHN B., *American Space: The Centennial Years,* New York: W. W. Norton and Company, Inc., 1972.

JAMES, G.A. and H. T. SCHREUDER, "Estimating Recreation Use of the San Gorgonio Wilderness," *Journal of Forestry,* Vol. 69, August 1971, pp. 490-493.

JAMES, WILLIAM, *The Varieties of Religious Experience,* London: Longmans, Green and Company, 1929 (37th impression; 1st edition June 1902).

JARRETT, HENRY (ed.), *Environmental Quality in a Growing Economy,* Baltimore: The Johns Hopkins University Press, for Resources for the Future, Inc., 1966.

JOHNSON, H. B., "The Appalachian Trail and Beyond," *American Institute of Architects Journal,* Vol. 56, October 1971, pp. 23-27.

JONES, R. A., "Fratricide in the Sierra Club," *Nation,* Vol. 208, May 5, 1969, pp. 567-570.

JUNG, C. G. (ed.), *Man and His Symbols,* New York: Dell, 1968.

KAUFFMAN, JOHN M., "A Place for a Park," *Journal of Forestry,* Vol. 66, July 1968, pp. 533-536.

KEPES, GYORGY, *The New Landscape in Art and Science,* Chicago: Paul Theobald and Company, 1956.

————, *Education of Vision,* New York: George Braziller, Inc., 1965.

KILGORE, BRUCE M. (ed.), *Wilderness in a Changing World: Proceedings, Ninth Biennial Wilderness Conference,* San Francisco: Sierra Club, 1966.

KOEHLER, R.E., "Ah, Wilderness," *American Institute of Architects Journal,* Vol. 49, February 1968, pp. 5-6.

KRUTCH, JOSEPH WOOD, *The Voice of the Desert: A Naturalist's Interpretation,* New York: William Sloane Associates, 1954.

_____, *Grand Canyon: Today and All Its Yesterdays*, New York: William Sloane Associates, 1962.

_____, *More Lives Than One*, New York: William Sloane Associates, 1962.

_____, *Baja California and the Geography of Hope*, San Francisco: Sierra Club, 1967.

_____, *The Best Nature Writing of Joseph Wood Krutch*, New York: William Morrow and Company, Inc., 1969.

_____, *A Krutch Omnibus: Forty Years of Social and Literary Criticism*, New York: William Morrow and Company, Inc., 1970.

LAMB, F.B., "Elements of Wilderness Management," *Journal of Forestry*, Vol. 71, September 1973, pp. 588-590.

LANGER, SUSANNE K., *Feeling and Form: A Theory of Art*, New York: Charles Scribner's Sons, 1953.

LAWSON, HERBERT G., "Critics Step Up Battle With Timber Industry Over Logging Methods," *Wall Street Journal*, January 24, 1974, pp. 1+.

LEADRABRAND, R., "Mineral King, Go or No Go?" *American Forests*, Vol. 75, October 1969, pp. 32-35.

LEE, DOUGLAS H.K., "Variability in Human Response to Arid Environments," in *Arid Lands in Perspective*, W.G. McGINNIES and B.J. GOLDMAN (eds.), Tucson: University of Arizona Press, 1969, pp. 227-245.

VAN DER LEEUW, GERARDUS, *Sacred and Profane Beauty: The Holy in Art*, New York: Holt, Rinehart and Winston, 1963.

_____, *Religion in Essence and Manifestation*, Vols. 1 and 2, Gloucester, Mass.: Peter Smith, 1967.

LEOPOLD, ALDO, *Round River: From the Journals of Aldo Leopold*, LUNA B. LEOPOLD (ed.), New York: Oxford University Press, 1953.

_____, *A Sand County Almanac and Sketches Here and There*, New York: Oxford University Press, 1969.

LEYDET, FRANCOIS (ed.), *Tomorrow's Wilderness: Proceedings of the 1963 Wilderness Conference*, San Francisco: Sierra Club, 1963.

LIME, DAVID and CHARLES T. CUSHWA, "The Aesthetic Importance of Wildlife to Auto Campers in the Superior National Forest," unpublished paper, North Central Forest Experiment Station, St. Paul, Minnesota.

Living Wilderness, "The Land Nobody Wanted," Vol. 31, No. 98, Autumn 1967, pp. 27-30.

LOWENTHAL, DAVID, "Is Wilderness 'Paradise Enow'? Images of Nature in America," *Columbia University Forum*, Vol. 7, No. 2, Spring 1964, pp. 34-40.

LUCAS, ROBERT C., "Trends in Use of the Boundary Waters Canoe Area and the National Wilderness Use Picture," text of a talk prepared for the Northwest Minnesota Chapter of the Society of American Foresters meeting, Grand Rapids, Minnesota, 1964.

_____, "Wilderness Perception and Use: The Example of the Boundary Waters Canoe Area," *Natural Resources Journal*, Vol. 3, 1964, pp. 394-411.

_____, "The Contribution of Environmental Research to Wilderness Policy Decisions," *The Journal of Social Issues*, Vol. 22, 1966, pp. 116-126.

_____, "Hikers and Other Trail Users," *Recreation Symposium Proceedings*, U.S. Forest Service, Northeast Forest Experiment Station, 1971.

_____ , "Natural Amenities, Outdoor Recreation, and Wilderness," in *Ecology, Economics, Environment,* R.W. ECHAN and RICHARD M. WEDDLE (eds.), Missoula, Mont.: Montana Forest and Conservation Experiment Station, School of Forestry, University of Montana, 1971, pp. 131-150.

McCLOSKEY, MAXINE E. (ed.), *Wilderness and the Quality of Life,* San Francisco: Sierra Club, 1969.

_____ , *Wilderness: The Edge of Knowledge,* San Francisco: Sierra Club, 1970.

McCOOL, STEPHEN F. and L.C. MERRIAM, JR., "Factors Associated with Littering Behavior in the Boundary Waters Canoe Area," Minnesota Forestry Research Note, No. 218, 1970.

McHARG, IAN, *Design With Nature,* Garden City, N.Y.: American Museum of Natural History, Natural History Press, 1969.

McPHEE, JOHN, *Encounters with the Archdruid,* New York: Farrar, Straus and Giroux, 1971.

MADDOCK, S. J., G.A. GEHRKEN, and W. A. GUTHRIE, *Rural Male Residents' Participation in Outdoor Recreation,* U.S. Forest Service Research Note, SE-49, 1965.

MARX, LEO, *The Machine in the Garden: Technology and the Pastoral Ideal in America,* New York: Oxford University Press, 1964.

MATROS, RONALD J., *Geography and the Aesthetic Landscape,* unpublished M.A. thesis, University of Minnesota, 1963.

MERRIAM, L.C. JR., "The Bob Marshall Wilderness in Montana—Some Socio-Economic Considerations," *Journal of Forestry,* Vol. 62, 1964, pp. 789-795.

MERRIAM, L. C. JR. and R.B. AMMONS, *The Wilderness User in Three Montana Areas,* St. Paul: School of Forestry, University of Minnesota, 1967.

MITCHELL, JOHN G. (ed.), *Ecotactics: The Sierra Club Handbook for Environmental Activists,* New York: Pocket Books, for the Sierra Club, 1970.

MORAN, JOSEPH M., MICHAEL D. MORGAN, and JAMES H. WIERSMA, *Environmental Analysis,* Green Bay, Wisc.: Little, Brown and Company, Inc., for the University of Wisconsin, Green Bay, 1971.

MUIR, JOHN, *Yosemite and the Sierra Nevadas,* selections from the works of John Muir, CHARLOTTE E. MAUK (ed.), photographs and introduction by ANSEL ADAMS, Boston: Houghton Mifflin Company, 1948.

NAGEL, ERNEST and JAMES R. NEWMAN, *Gödel's Proof,* New York: New York University Press, 1964.

NASH, RODERICK, *Wilderness and the American Mind,* New Haven: Yale University Press, 1967.

_____ , (ed.), *The Call of the Wild: 1900-1916,* New York: George Braziller, 1970.

NEWHALL, NANCY, *Ansel Adams: The Eloquent Light,* San Francisco: Sierra Club, 1963.

New Republic, "Conservationists and the IRS, Vol. 155, December 3, 1966, p. 7.

Newsweek, "Battle for the Wilderness," Vol. 68, October 3, 1966, p. 108.

_____ , "Fall From Grace," Vol. 69, January 9, 1967, pp. 24-25.

_____ , "Fighting Sierrans," Vol. 70, December 25, 1967, p. 50.

_____ , "Mom vs. Apple Pie; Opposes Disney's Proposed Alpine Village," Vol. 73, February 10, 1969, p. 25.

New York Times, "Financial Troubles in Sierra Club," February 20, 1972, p. 3.

New Yorker, "Books: Briefly Noted Fiction," Vol. 44, No. 7, April 6, 1968, pp. 174-175.

NICHOLSON, MARJORIE HOPE, *Mountain Gloom and Mountain Glory: The Development of the Aesthetics of the Infinite*, Ithaca, N. Y.: Cornell University Press, 1959.

NIENABER, J., "Supreme Court and Mickey Mouse; Mineral King Case," *American Forests*, Vol. 78, July 1972, pp. 28-31+.

OTTO, RUDOLPH, *The Idea of the Holy: An Inquiry Into the Idea of the Divine and Its Relation to the Rational*, London: Oxford University Press, 1925.

PETERSON, H., "Brower Power Awaits the Verdict," *Sports Illustrated*, Vol. 30, April 14, 1969, pp. 36-38+.

POMEROY, EARL, *In Search of the Golden West: The Tourist in Western America*, New York: Alfred A. Knopf, 1957.

PORTER, ELIOT, *Galapagos: The Flow of Wildness*, San Francisco: Sierra Club, 1968.

Publisher's Weekly, "Sierra Club's Thoreau Book Marks Expanding Program," Vol. 182, October 1, 1962, pp. 78+.

_____ , "Sierra Club's Future Publishing Plans," Vol. 197, February 2, 1970, p. 68.

_____ , New Sierra Books to Feature People," Vol. 201, March 6, 1972, p. 49.

ROBERTS, ARTHUR M., "A Forestry Association's View of the Proposals," *Journal of Forestry*, Vol. 66, July 1968, pp. 521-526.

ROSENWEIG, PAUL J., *The Wilderness in American Fiction: A Psycho-Analytic Study of a Central American Myth*, unpublished Ph.D. dissertation, University of Michigan, 1972.

RUDROUF, LUCIEN, "Perfection," *Journal of Aesthetics and Art Criticism*, Vol. 23, No. 1, Fall 1964, pp. 123-130.

SCHMITT, PETER J., *Back to Nature: The Arcadian Myth in Urban America*, New York: Oxford University Press, 1969.

SCHWARTZ, WILLIAM (ed.), *Voices for the Wilderness*, New York: Ballantine Books, 1964.

SEMPLE, ELLEN CHURCHILL, *Influences of Geographic Environment*, New York: H. Holt and Company, 1911.

SHEPARD, PAUL, *Man in the Landscape: A Historic View of the Aesthetics of Nature*, New York: Alfred A. Knopf, 1967.

Sierra Club, *Sierra Club Bulletin*, San Francisco, June 1899-November 1973.

SIMONDS, JOHN E., "Symms Loses Fight to Delay Hell's Canyon Action," *Idaho Statesman*, September 11, 1975, p. 1+.

SNYDER, A.P., "Wilderness Management: A Growing Challenge," *Journal of Forestry*, Vol. 64, July 1966, pp. 441-446.

SONNERFIELD, J., "Variable Values in Space and Landscape: An Inquiry into the Nature of Environmental Necessity," *Journal of Social Issues*, Vol. 22, 1966, pp. 71-82.

SPURNY, M. and P. MAZAL, "On Landscape Photography: An Attempt to Free Landscape Photography from Extreme Aestheticism of Form," *Camera*, Vol. 44, August 1965, pp. 17-23.

STANKEY, GEORGE H., "A Strategy for the Definition and Management of Wilderness Quality," in *Natural Environments: Studies in Theoretical and Applied Analysis*, JOHN V. KRUTILLA (ed.), Baltimore: The Johns Hopkins University Press, 1972, pp. 88-114.

STEIN, ROGER B., *John Ruskin and Aesthetic Thought in America, 1840-1900*, Cambridge, Mass.: Harvard University Press, 1967.

STONE, HERBERT J., "Forest or Park? A Former Regional Forester's View," *Journal of Forestry*, Vol. 66, July 1968, pp. 527-532.

SULLIVAN, MICHAEL, *The Birth of Landscape Painting in China*, Berkeley: University of California Press, 1962.

SZARKOWSKI, JOHN, "The Photographer and the American Landscape," *Art in America*, May 1963, pp. 52-55.

TEALE, EDWIN WAY, "Making the Wild Scene," *The New York Times Review*, January 28, 1968, p. 7.

THURBER, S.,"Conservation Comes of Age; California Movement," *Nation*, Vol. 204, February 27, 1967, pp. 272-275.

Time, "Call of the Wild," Vol. 83, March 27, 1964, p. 54.

_____, "Disrupting Disney: Suit Against Mineral King Resort," Vol. 99, May 1, 1972, p. 62.

_____, "Anger in Alaska: Movement for Independence," Vol. 102, August 20, 1973, p. 57.

TUAN, YI-FU, *Man and Nature*, Washington D.C.: Association of American Geographers, Commission on College Geography, 1971.

_____, *Topophilia: A Study of Environmental Perception, Attitudes, and Values*, Englewood Cliffs, N.J.: Prentice-Hall, Inc., 1974.

_____, "Geopiety: A Theme in Man's Attachment to Nature and Place," in *Geographies of the Mind: Essays in Historical Geography in Honor of John Kirtland Wright*, DAVID LOWENTHAL and MARTYN J. BOWDEN (eds.), New York: Oxford University Press, 1975, pp. 11-39.

United States Forest Service, *National Forest Wilderness and Primitive Areas*, Washington, D.C.: Government Printing Office, 1968.

UPTON, JOHN, "Review of Two Books of Photos by Eliot Porter," *Aperture*, Vol. 2, No. 2, February 1964, pp. 82-83.

VALE, T.R., "Objectivity, Values, and the Redwoods," *Landscape*, Vol. 19, Winter 1970, pp. 30-33.

WALEY, ARTHUR, *An Introduction to the Study of Chinese Painting*, New York: Grove Press, Inc., 1958 (1st printing 1923).

WATSON, R., "Festival in Washington," *Christian Century*, Vol. 89, January 26, 1972, p. 104.

WAZEKA, ROBERT T., *The Solitary Escape in Recent American Literature*, unpublished Ph.D. dissertation, University of Colorado, 1971.

WEBER, DANIEL B., *John Muir: The Function of Wilderness in an Industrial Society*, unpublished Ph.D. dissertation, University of Minnesota, 1964.

WERNICK, R., "Spoiling for a Good Fight," *Holiday*, Vol. 44, December 1968, pp. 58-59.

WHITE, MINOR, "The Photographer and the American Landscape," *Aperture*, Vol. 2, No. 2, February 1964, pp. 52-55.

WHITTAKER, JIM (ed.), "Lake Melakwa Clean-up Proves Successful," *Viewpoint*, Vol. 2, September 1973, Seattle: Recreational Equipment, Inc., pp. 21-24.

WILDAVSKY, A., "Aesthetic Power, or the Triumph of the Sensitive Minority Over the Vulgar Mass: A Political Analysis of the New Economics," *Daedalus*, Fall 1967, pp. 1115-1128.

WILLIAMS, GEORGE H., *Wilderness and Paradise in Christian Thought*, New York: Harper and Brothers, 1962.

WILLIAMS, RAYMOND, *The Country and the City*, New York: Oxford University Press, 1973.